GERMAN

in 10 minutes a day®

by **Kristine Kershul**, M.A., University of California, Santa Barbara

A Sunset Series

Lane Publishing Co.
Menlo Park, CA 94025

P9-CFO-682

Third printing October 1988

 ISBN 0-944502-19-9.
Lithographed in the United States.

(ahl-fah-bate)
das Alphabet

Many German letters sound the same as in English, but some German letters are pronounced or written differently. To learn the German sounds of these letters, write each example in the space provided. After you practice each word, see if you can locate it on the map.

German letter	English sound	Example	*Write it here*
a	ah	**Hamburg** *(hahm-boorg)*	Hamburg
ä	ay	**Dänemark** *(day-nah-mark)*	Dänemark
au	ow/au	**Passau** *(pahs-sau)*	Passau
äu/eu	oy	**Europa** *(oy-roh-pah)*	Europa
ch	hk *(breathe hard)*	**Frankreich** *(frahnk-reihk)*	Frankreich
e *(varies)*	ay *or* eh	**Bremen** *(bray-men)*	Bremen
ei	eye/ai/i	**Rhein** *(rine)*	Rhein
er	air	**Berlin** *(bair-leen)*	Berlin
i	ih	**Inn** *(in)*	Inn
ie	ee	**Kiel** *(keel)*	Kiel
o	oh	**Polen** *(poh-len)*	Polen
ö	ur	**Köln** *(kurln)*	Köln
qu	kv	**Marquartstein** *(mar-kvart-shtine)*	Marquartstein
r	*(slightly rolled)*	**Rostock** *(roh-shtoke)*	Rostock
s *(varies)*	s *or* z	**Ostsee** *(ohst-zay)*	
sch	sh	**Schweden** *(shvay-den)*	
ß	ss	**Meßstetten** *(mess-shtet-en)*	
th	t	**Gotha** *(go-tah)*	
u	oo	**Ulm** *(oolm)*	Ulm
ü	ew/ue	**München** *(mewn-shen)*	
v	f	**Hannover** *(hahn-noh-fair)*	
w	v	**Weimar** *(vie-mar)*	
z	ts	**Koblenz** *(koh-blents)*	
e *(end of word)*	ah	**Elbe** *(el-bah)*	

Now practice the important words you learned on the inside front cover.

(vahs) *(ine-ah)* *(bah-nah-nah)*
Was ist das? Das ist eine Banane.
what is that a banana

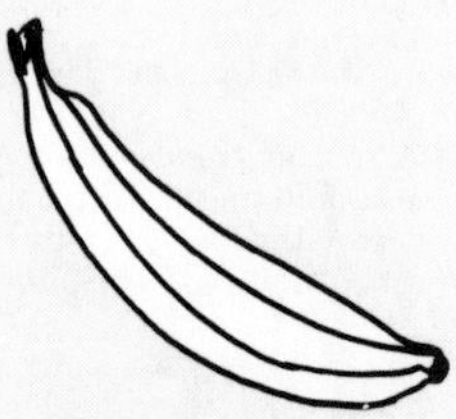

(eehk) *(murk-tah)* *(ine-ah)*
Ich möchte eine Banane.
I would like

(vahs) *(ine)* *(beer)*
Was ist das? Das ist ein Bier.
a beer

Ich möchte ein Bier.

Seven Key Question Words

When you arrive in the *(boon-des-ray-poo-bleek)* **Bundesrepublik** (Federal Republic) *(doych-lahnt)* **Deutschland,** (Germany) the very first thing you will need to do is to ask questions— "Where is the train station?" "Where can I exchange money?" "Where *(voh)* (**wo**) is the lavatory?" "**Wo** is a restaurant?" "**Wo** do I catch a taxi?" "**Wo** is a good hotel?" "**Wo** is my luggage?"—and the list will go on and on for the entire length of your visit. In German, there are SEVEN KEY QUESTION WORDS to learn. For example, the seven key question words will help you to find out exactly what you are ordering in a restaurant before you order it—and not after the surprise (or shock!) arrives. These seven basic question words all begin with "**w**" (which is pronounced like "v").

Take a few minutes to study and practice saying the seven basic question words listed below. Then cover the German words with your hand and fill in each of the blanks with the matching German *(vort)* **Wort** (word).

1.	*(voh)* **WO**	=	WHERE	wo, wo, wo, wo
2.	*(vahs)* **WAS**	=	WHAT	______
3.	*(vair)* **WER**	=	WHO	______
4.	*(vah-room)* **WARUM**	=	WHY	______
5.	*(vahn)* **WANN**	=	WHEN	______
6.	*(vee)* **WIE**	=	HOW	______
7.	*(vee-feel)* **WIEVIEL**	=	HOW MUCH	______

Now test yourself to see if you really can keep these **Wörter** (vur-tair) (words) straight in your mind. Draw lines between the German **und** (oont) (and) English equivalents below.

why	**wer**
what	**was**
who	**wo**
how	**wieviel**
where	**wann**
when	**warum**
how much	**wie**

Examine the following questions containing these **Wörter** (vur-tair). Practice the sentences out loud **und** (oont) then quiz yourself by filling in the blanks below with the correct question **Wort** (vort).

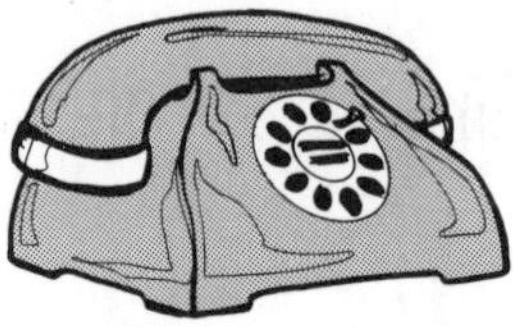

(voh) (ist) (ine) (tay-lay-fohn)
Wo ist ein Telefon?
Where is a telephone?

(vair) (dahs)
Wer ist das?
Who is that?

(vahn) (kohmt) (dair) (tsook)
Wann kommt der Zug?
When comes the train?

(vee-feel) (koh-stet)
Wieviel kostet das?
How much costs this?

(vahs) (lohs)
Was ist los?
What is wrong?

(vee) (dair) (zah-laht)
Wie ist der Salat?
How is the salad?

(vahn) (kohmt) (mahn)
Wann kommt der Mann?
When comes the man?

(vah-room) (neehkt)
Warum kommt der Zug nicht?
Why comes the train not?

1. ____________ **ist der Salat?**
2. ____________ **kostet das?**
3. ____________ **ist los?**
4. ____________ **ist ein Telefon?**
5. ____________ **kommt der Zug nicht?**
6. Wer **ist das?**
7. ____________ **kommt der Zug?**
8. ____________ **kommt der Mann?**

Wo (voh) will be your most used question **Wort** (vort) so let's concentrate on it. Say each of the following German sentences aloud. Then write out each sentence without looking at the example. If you don't succeed on the first try, don't give up. Just practice each sentence until you are able to do it easily.

Don't forget that you pronounce "ei" like "eye" **und** "ie" like "ee." Also, in German you pronounce every letter you see.

(voh) (ine-ah) (toy-let-tah)
Wo ist eine Toilette?

(ine) (tahx-ee)
Wo ist ein Taxi?

(boos)
Wo ist ein Bus?

Wo ist eine Toilette? ____________________ ____________________

(res-toh-rahnt)
Wo ist ein Restaurant?

(ine-ah) (bahnk)
Wo ist eine Bank?

(ine)
Wo ist ein Hotel?

____________________ ____________________ ____________________

Ja *(yah)* (yes), many of the **Wörter** *(vur-tair)* which look like **Englisch** *(eng-leash)* (English) are also **Deutsch** *(doych)* (German). Since **Deutsch und** *(oont)* **Englisch** are related languages, your work here **ist** simpler. You will be amazed at the number of **Wörter** which are identical (or almost identical). Of course, they do not always sound the same when spoken by a German, but the similarity will certainly surprise you. Listed below are five "free" **Wörter** beginning with "A" to help you get started. Be sure to say each **Wort** *(vort)* aloud **und** *(oont)* then write out the German **Wort** in the blank to the right.

- ☐ **die Adresse** *(ah-dress-sah)*............ the address ____________________
- ☐ **das Amerika** *(ah-mair-ih-kah)*......... America ____________________
- ☐ **der April** *(ah-pril)*.................. April ____________________
- ☐ **der August** *(ow-goost)*................ August ____________________
- ☐ **das Auto** *(ow-toh)*.................... the car/automobile ____________________

Free **Wörter** like these will appear at the bottom of the following pages in a yellow color band. Check them off as you learn them. They are easy—enjoy them!

Step 2

"the"

All of these words mean "the" *(owf)* **auf** *(doych)* **Deutsch:** German

(dair) **der**	*(dee)* **die**	*(dahs)* **das**	*(dain)* **den**	*(dehm)* **dem**	*(des)* **des**

(mahn) **der Mann:** the man

(frow) **die Frau:** the woman

(kint) **das Kind:** the child

(fah-tair) **den Vater:** the father

(froy-line) **dem Fräulein:** the young woman

(ow-toes) **des Autos:** the car

"a" or "an"

All of these words mean "a" or "an":

(ine) **ein**	*(ine-ah)* **eine**	*(ine-in)* **einen**	*(ine-air)* **einer**	*(ine-em)* **einem**	*(ine-es)* **eines**

ein Mann: a man

eine Frau: a woman

ein Kind: a child

einem Vater: a father

einem Fräulein: a young girl

eines Autos: a car

(doych) **Deutsch** German has multiple *(vur-tair)* **Wörter** for "the" *(oont)* **und** "a," but there **ist** no need to worry about it. Just make a choice **und** remember to use one of these **Wörter** when you mean "the" *(oh-dair)* **oder** or "a."

Step 3

(ding-ah) die Dinge

things

Before you proceed **mit** with this step, situate yourself comfortably in your living room. Now look around you. Can you name the things which you see in this *(tsi-mair)* **Zimmer** room in German? Probably you can guess *(dahs) (zoh-fah)* **das Sofa** and maybe even *(dee) (lahm-pah)* **die Lampe**. Let's learn the rest of them. After practicing these *(vur-tair)* **Wörter** out loud, write them in the blanks below **und** on the next page.

(bilt) **das Bild** = the picture das Bild

(dee) (deck-ah) **die Decke** = the ceiling ____________________

- ☑ **der Amerikaner** *(ah-mair-ih-kahn-air)*.. the American ____________
- ☐ **der Apfel** *(ahp-fel)*.................... the apple ____________
- ☐ **der Appetit** *(ah-pe-teet)*.............. the appetite ____________
- ☐ **der Akzent** *(ahk-tsent)*................ the accent ____________
- ☐ **das Afrika** *(ah-fri-kah)*............... Africa ____________

(dee) (eck-ah)
die Ecke = the corner ______________________

(dahs) (fen-stair)
das Fenster = the window ______________________

(lahm-pah)
die Lampe = the lamp ______________________

(leeht)
das Licht = the light ______________________

(zoh-fah)
das Sofa = the sofa ______________________

(dair) (shtool)
der Stuhl = the chair ______________________

(tep-eeh)
der Teppich = the carpet ______________________

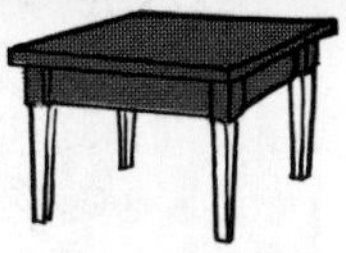

(tish)
der Tisch = the table ______________________

(tewr)
die Tür = the door die Tür

(uhr)
die Uhr = the clock ______________________

(for-hahng)
der Vorhang = the curtain ______________________

(vahnt)
die Wand = the wall ______________________

You will notice that the correct form of **der, die, oder das** *(dair) (dee) (oh-dair)(dahs)* is given **mit** (with) each noun. This is for your information—just remember to use one of them. Open your book to the sticky labels (between pages 48 and 49). Peel off the first 14 labels **und** proceed around the **Zimmer,** *(tsi-mair)* labeling these items in your home. This will help to increase your **deutsche Wort** *(doy-chah)* power easily. Don't forget to say **das Wort** *(vort)* as you attach each label.

Now ask yourself, **,,Wo ist das Bild?"** *(voh) (bilt)* **und** point at it while you answer, **,,Dort ist das Bild."** (there)

Continue on down the list until you feel comfortable with these new **Wörter**. Say, "**Wo ist die** *(dee)* **Decke**?" Then reply, "**Dort ist die Decke**," and so on. When you can identify all the items on the list, you will be ready to move on.

Now, starting on the next page, let's learn some basic parts of the house.

- ☐ **der Akt** *(ahkt)* . . . . act (of a play) ______________
- ☐ **die Akademie** *(ah-kah-dih-mee)* . . . . the academy ______________
- ☐ **der Alkohol** *(ahl-koh-hole)* . . . . the alcohol ______________
- ☐ **alle** *(ahl-lah)* . . . . all ______________
- ☐ **der Autor** *(ow-tohr)* . . . . the author ______________

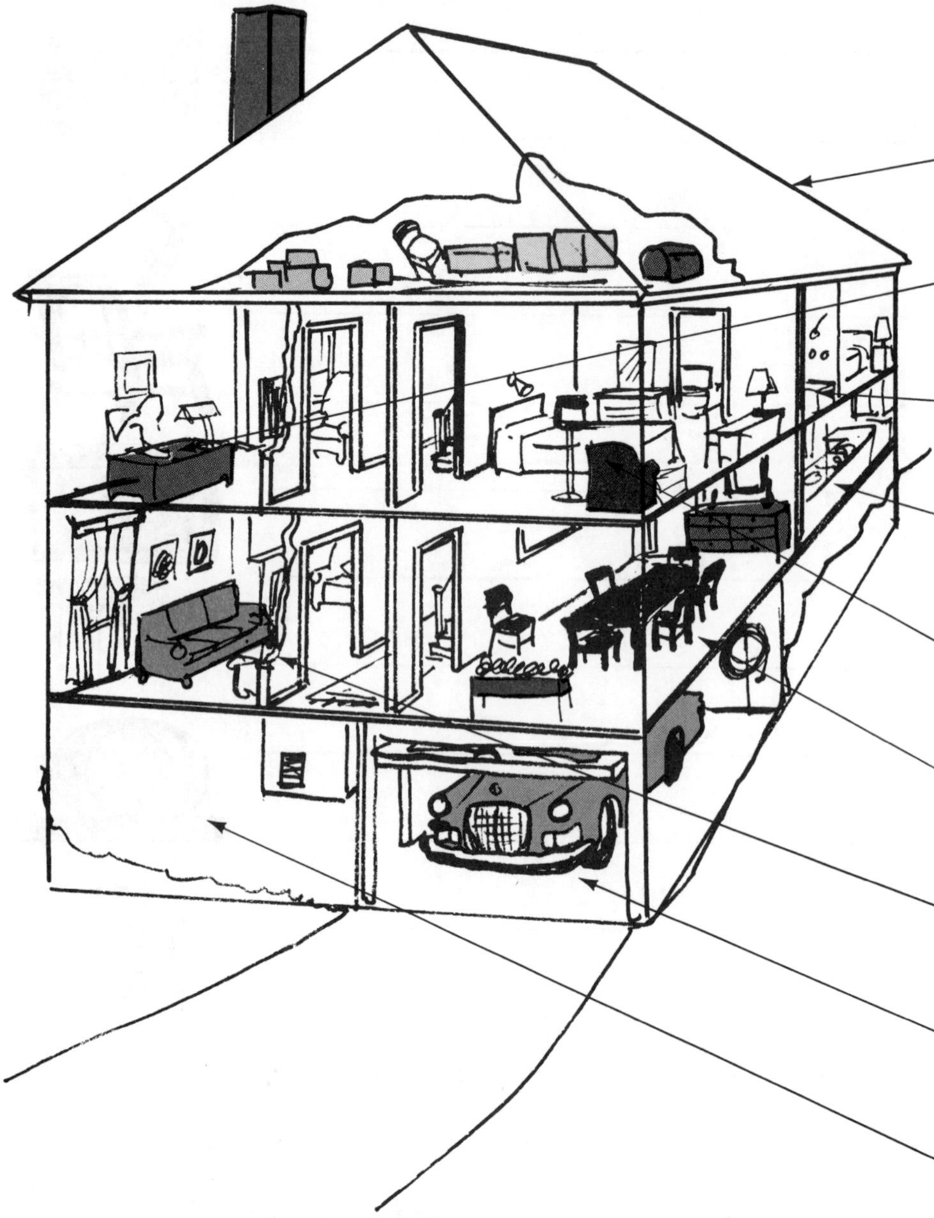

das Haus *(house)* = the house

Dort ist das Haus *(house)*.

das Büro *(bew-roh)* office / study

das Badezimmer *(bah-da-tsi-mair)* bathroom

die Küche *(kew-sha)* kitchen

das Schlafzimmer *(shlahf-tsi-mair)* bedroom

das Eßzimmer *(es-tsi-mair)* dining room

das Wohnzimmer *(vohn-tsi-mair)* living room

die Garage *(ga-rah-zha)* garage

der Keller *(kel-lair)* basement

While learning these new **Wörter** *(vur-tair)*, let's not forget

das Auto *(ow-toe)* **/ der Wagen** *(vah-gen)*

das Fahrrad *(fahr-raht)*

der Hund *(hoont)*

das Auto/der Wagen ____________ ____________

- ☐ **der Bäcker** *(beck-air)*................ the baker ____________
- ☐ **die Bäckerei** *(beck-air-eye)*........... the bakery ____________
- ☐ **der Ball** *(bahl)*...................... the ball ____________
- ☐ **das Ballett** *(bah-let)*................ the ballet ____________
- ☐ **die Banane** *(ba-nah-nah)*.............. the banana ____________

die Katze *(kaht-tsa)*

der Garten *(gar-ten)*

die Post *(post)*

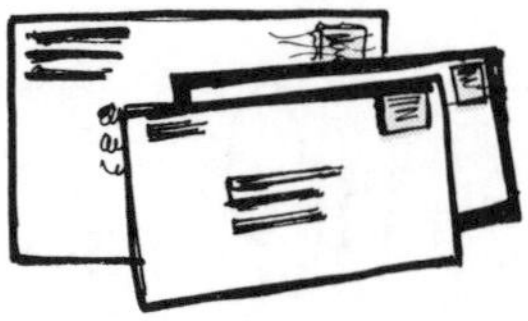

die Post

der Briefkasten *(breef-kah-sten)*
mail box

die Blumen *(bloo-men)*
flowers

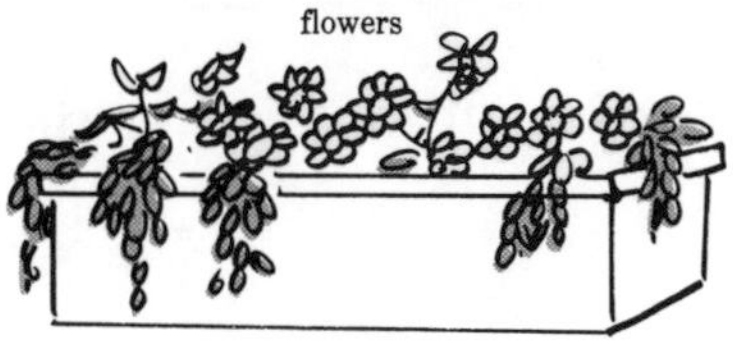

die Klingel *(kling-el)*
door bell

Peel off the next set of labels **und** *(oont)* wander through your **Haus** *(house)* learning these new **Wörter** *(vur-tair)*. Granted, it will be somewhat difficult to label your **Hund** *(hoont)*, **Katze**, **oder** *(oh-dair)* **die Blumen** *(bloo-men)*, but use your imagination.

Again, practice by asking yourself, **„Wo** *(voh)* **ist der** *(dair)* **Garten** *(gar-ten)***?“** and reply, **„Dort ist der Garten.“**

Now for the following:

Wo ist...

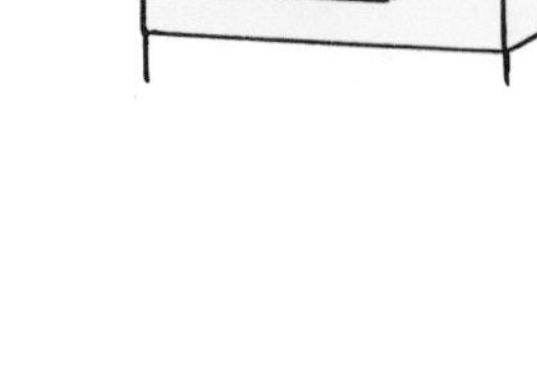

- ☐ **die Bank** *(bahnk)* .... the bank
- ☐ **das Beefsteak** *(beef-steak)* .... the steak
- ☐ **das Bett** *(bet)* .... the bed
- ☐ **besser** *(bess-air)* .... better
- ☐ **das Bier** *(beer)* .... beer

Step 4

Eins, zwei, g'suffa! *(ines) (tsvai) (ge-zoo-fah)*
one, two, drink

„In München steht ein Hofbräuhaus, Eins, zwei, g'suffa!"
(mewn-shen) (sh-tayt) (ine) (hohf-broy-house)
In Munich stands a brewery one two drink

When one thinks of **deutsche** *(doy-chah)* **Bier** *(beer)*-drinking songs, this **ist** one of the most famous. The **Hofbräuhaus** *(hohf-broy-house)* **ist** still to be found **in München** *(mewn-shen)* **und ist** an experience to visit. Let's learn how to join in on the refrain of **„Eins, zwei, g'suffa!"** *(ines) (tsvai) (ge-zoo-fah)* This **ist** where you are given a chance to swing your **Bier** stein once to the left **(eins)**, once to the right **(zwei)**, **und** then **es ist** time to take a drink **(g'suffa)**: **Eins, zwei, g'suffa!** When learning the following **Nummern** *(noo-mairn)* (numbers), notice the similarities (underlined) between **vier** *(fear)* (4) **und vierzehn** *(fear-tsayn)* (14), **fünf** *(fewnf)* (5) **und fünfzehn** *(fewnf-tsayn)* (15) **und** so on. After practicing **die Wörter** *(vur-tair)* out loud, cover the **Deutsch** *(doych)* **und** write out **die Nummern** 1 through 10 in the blanks.

0	**null** *(nool)*			0	null
1	**eins** *(ines)*	11	**elf** *(elf)*	1	______
2	**zwei** *(tsvai)*	12	**zwölf** *(ts-vurlf)*	2	______
3	**drei** *(dry)*	13	**dreizehn** *(dry-tsayn)*	3	______
4	**vier** *(fear)*	14	**vierzehn** *(fear-tsayn)*	4	______
5	**fünf** *(fewnf)*	15	**fünfzehn** *(fewnf-tsayn)*	5	______
6	**sechs** *(zex)*	16	**sechzehn** *(zex-tsayn)*	6	______
7	**sieben** *(zee-ben)*	17	**siebzehn** *(zeep-tsayn)*	7	______
8	**acht** *(ahkt)*	18	**achtzehn** *(ahkt-tsayn)*	8	______
9	**neun** *(noyn)*	19	**neunzehn** *(noyn-tsayn)*	9	______
10	**zehn** *(tsayn)*	20	**zwanzig** *(tsvahn-tsig)*	10	______

- ☐ **blau** *(blau)* .... blue ______
- ☐ **das Boot** *((boht)*.................... the boat ______
- ☐ **braun** *(brown)* .... brown ______
- ☐ **bringen** *(bring-in)* .... to bring ______
- ☐ **die Butter** *(boo-tair)*............... the butter ______

Use these **Nummern** *(noo-mairn)* on a daily basis. Count to yourself **auf** *(owf)* in **Deutsch** *(doych)* German when you brush your teeth, exercise, **oder** *(oh-dair)* commute to work. Now fill in the following blanks according to the **Nummern** *(noo-mairn)* given in parentheses.

Note: This is a good time to start learning these **zwei** *(tsvai)* important phrases.

Ich möchte *(eehk) (murk-tah)*	=	I would like	______________
wir möchten *(vir) (murk-ten)*	=	we would like	______________

Ich möchte *(eehk)* ______________ (15)	**Stück Papier.** *(shtewk) (pah-peer)* pieces of paper	**Wieviel?** *(vee-feel)* ______________ (15)
Ich möchte ______________ (10)	**Postkarten.** *(post-kar-ten)* postcards 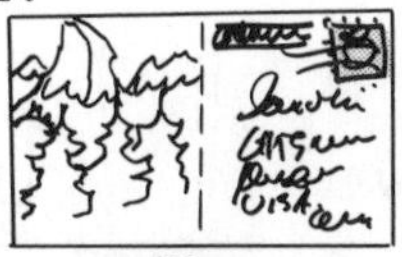	**Wieviel?** ______________ (10)
Ich möchte ______________ (11)	**Briefmarken.** *(breef-mar-ken)* stamps 	**Wieviel?** ______________ (11)
Ich möchte ______________ (8)	**Liter Benzin.** *(lee-tair) (ben-tseen)* liters of gas	**Wieviel?** acht (8)
Ich möchte ______________ (1)	**Glas Orangensaft.** *(glahs) (oh-rahn-zhen-zahft)* glass of orange juice 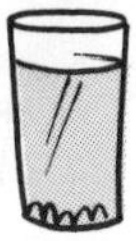	**Wieviel?** ______________ (1)
Wir möchten *(vir)* ______________ (3)	**Tassen Tee.** *(tah-sen) (tay)* cups of tea	**Wieviel?** ______________ (3)
Wir möchten vier (4)	**Theaterkarten.** *(tay-ah-tair-kar-ten)* theater tickets 	**Wieviel?** ______________ (4)
Wir möchten ______________ (2)	**Bier.** *(beer)* beer 	**Wieviel?** ______________ (2)
Ich möchte *(eehk)* ______________ (12)	**frische Eier.** *(frish-ah) (eye-air)* fresh eggs	**Wieviel?** ______________ (12)
Wir möchten *(vir)* ______________ (6)	**Pfund Fleisch.** *(foont) (flaisch)* pounds of meat	**Wieviel?** ______________ (6)
Wir möchten ______________ (5)	**Glas Wasser.** *(vah-sair)* glasses of water 	**Wieviel?** ______________ (5)
Ich möchte *(eehk)* ______________ (7)	**Glas Wein.** *(vine)* glasses of wine 	**Wieviel?** ______________ (7)
Wir möchten *(vir)* ______________ (9)	**Pfund Butter.** *(foont) (boo-tair)* pounds of butter 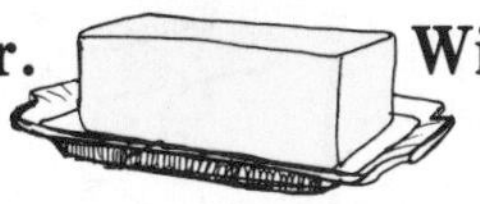	**Wieviel?** ______________ (9)

Deutsch itself actually has no "C's," so you will note that all of these free **Wörter** are taken into **Deutsch** from other languages.

- ☐ **das Cafe** *(kah-fay)*.................... cafe ______________
- ☐ **der Champagner** *(shahm-pan-yair)*..... champagne ______________
- ☐ **die Chemie** *(shay-mee)*............... chemistry ______________

Now see if you can translate the following thoughts into *(doych)* **Deutsch.** The answers are at the bottom of the *(zigh-tah)* **Seite.** (page)

1. I would like 7 postcards. 

   ____

2. I would like 1 beer.  Ich möchte ein Bier.

3. We would like 2 glasses of water. 

   ____

4. We would like 3 theater tickets. 

   ____

Review **die** *(noo-mairn)* **Nummern** 1 through 20 *(oont)* **und** answer the following questions aloud, **und** then write the *(ahnt-vor-ten)* **Antworten** (answers) in the blank spaces.

(vee-feel) **Wieviel** *(tish-ah)* **Tische** *(zint)* **sind** (are) *(here)* **hier?**  ______________

Wieviel *(lahm-pen)* **Lampen sind hier?**  ______________

Wieviel *(shtewl-ah)* **Stühle sind hier?** 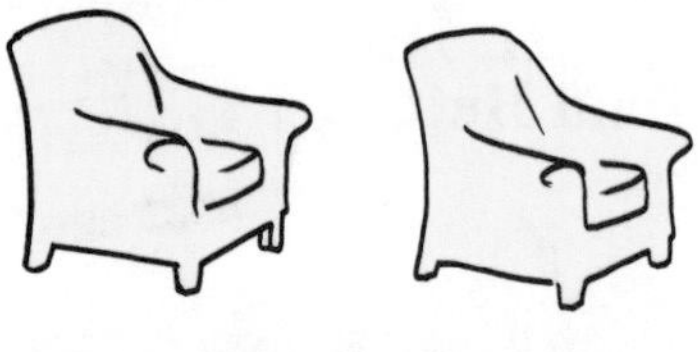 ______________

ANTWORTEN

1. **Ich möchte sieben Postkarten.**
2. **Ich möchte ein Bier.**
3. **Wir möchten zwei Glas Wasser.**
4. **Wir möchten drei Theaterkarten.**

Wieviel **Uhren** *(uhr-en)* **sind** *(zint)* **hier?**  ______________

Wieviel **Fenster** *(fen-stair)* **sind hier?** 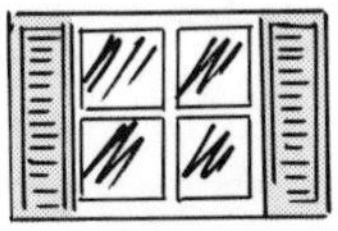 ______________

Wieviel **Personen** *(pair-zoh-nen)* **sind hier?**  sechs

Wieviel **Männer** *(men-air)* **sind hier?** ______________

Wieviel **Frauen** *(frow-en)* **sind hier?** ______________

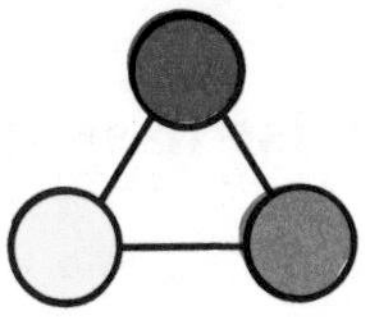

die *(dee)* **Farben** *(fahr-ben)* — colors

Step 5

Colors **sind** *(zint)* (are) the same **in Deutschland** *(doych-lahnt)* as **in Amerika** *(ah-mair-ih-kah)* — they just have different **Namen** *(nah-men)* (names). You can easily recognize **violett** *(vee-oh-let)* as violet **oder purpur** *(pur-pur)* as purple. So when you are invited to someone's **Haus** *(house)* **und** you want to bring flowers, you will be able to order the correct color of flowers. (Contrary to American custom, **in Europa** *(oy-roh-pah)* (Europe) **rote** *(roh-tah)* **Blumen** *(bloo-men)* (flowers), **und** particularly **rote Rosen** *(roh-zen)* (roses), are only exchanged between lovers!) Let's learn the basic **Farben** *(fahr-ben)*. Once you have read through **die** *(dee)* (the) **Liste** *(lis-tah)* (list) on the next **Seite,** *(zigh-tah)* cover the **Deutsch** *(doych)* **mit** (with) your **Hand,** *(hahnt)* **und** practice writing out the **Deutsch** next to the **Englisch.** *(eng-leash)* Notice the similarities (underlined) between the **deutsche** *(doy-chah)* **und** the **englische** *(eng-leash-ah)* (English) **Wörter.**

- ☐ **das Chile** *(she-lay)* . . . . Chile ______________
- ☐ **das China** *(she-nah)* . . . . China ______________
- ☐ **chinesisch** *(shi-nay-zish)* . . . . Chinese ______________
- ☐ **der Chor** *(core)* . . . . the choir ______________
- ☐ **christlich** *(krist-leeh)* . . . . christian ______________

weiß *(vice)* = white ________________ **Das Boot** *(boht)* **ist weiß.**

schwarz *(shvarts)* = black ________________ **Der Ball** *(bahl)* **ist schwarz.**

gelb *(gelp)* = yellow ________________ **Die Banane** *(bah-nah-nah)* **ist gelb.**

rot *(roht)* = red ________________ **Das Buch** *(boohk)* **ist rot.**

blau *(blau)* = blue blau ________________ **Das Auto** *(ow-toh)* **ist blau.**

grau *(grau)* = gray ________________ **Der Elefant** *(ay-lay-fahnt)* **ist grau.**

braun *(brown)* = brown ________________ **Der Stuhl** *(shtool)* **ist braun.**

grün *(grewn)* = green ________________ **Das Gras** *(grahs)* **ist grün.**

rosa *(roh-zah)* = pink ________________ **Die Blume** *(bloo-mah)* **ist rosa.**

bunt *(boont)* = multi-colored ________________ **Die Lampe** *(lahm-pah)* **ist bunt.**

Now peel off the next **zehn** *(tsayn)* labels **und** *(oont)* proceed to label these **Farben in** your **Haus.**

Now let's practice using these **Wörter.**

Wo *(voh)* **ist das weiße** *(vice-ah)* **Boot?** *(boht)* **Dort ist das** weiße **Boot.**

Wo ist der graue *(grau-ah)* **Tisch?** *(tish)* **Dort ist der** ________ **Tisch.**

Wo ist der braune *(brown-ah)* **Stuhl?** *(shtool)* **Dort ist der** ________ **Stuhl.**

Wo ist der weiße *(vice-ah)* **Ball?** *(bahl)* **Dort ist der** ________ **Ball.**

Wo ist die bunte *(boon-tah)* **Lampe?** *(lahm-pah)* **Dort ist die** ________ **Lampe.**

Wo ist das rote *(roh-tah)* **Buch?** *(boohk)* **Dort ist das** ________ **Buch.**

☐ **der Dezember** *(day-tsem-bair)*......... December ________________
☐ **der Doktor** *(dohk-tor)*................ the doctor ________________
— The doctor is a title; **der Arzt ist** the word for a medical doctor.
☐ **die Drogerie** *(droh-gih-ree)*........... the drugstore ________________

(grewn-ah) (tewr)
Wo ist die grüne Tür? **Dort ist die** ________ **Tür.**

(roh-zah) (house)
Wo ist das rosa Haus? **Dort ist das** ________ **Haus.**

(gel-bah) (bah-nah-nah)
Wo ist die gelbe Banane? **Dort ist die** ________ **Banane.**

(owf) (doych) (hah-ben)
Note: **Auf Deutsch** (In German) the verb for "to have" **ist „haben."**

(eehk) (hah-bah) **ich habe** = I have ____________________ *(vir)* **wir haben** = we have ____________________

(murk-ten) (hah-ben)
Let's review **möchten und** learn **haben**. Be sure to repeat each sentence out loud.

(eehk) (murk-tah) (glahs)
Ich möchte ein Glas Bier.

(hah-bah)
Ich habe ein Glas Bier.

(vir) (tsvai) (vine)
Wir möchten zwei Glas Wein.

(hah-ben)
Wir haben zwei Glas Wein.

(vah-sair)
Ich möchte ein Glas Wasser.

Wir haben ein Haus.

(zah-laht)
Wir möchten einen Salat.

(ah-mair-ih-kah)
Ich habe ein Haus in Amerika.

(ow-toe)
Wir möchten ein Auto.

Ich habe ein Auto.

(oy-roh-pah)
Wir möchten ein Auto in Europa.

Wir haben ein Auto in Europa.

Now fill in the following blanks **mit** the correct form of **„haben" oder „möchten."**

Wir haben ____________________ *(dry) (ow-toes)* **drei Autos.**
(we have)

____________________ *(tsvai)* **zwei Theaterkarten.**
(we would like)

____________________ *(bilt)* **ein Bild.**
(I have)

____________________ *(zee-ben)* **sieben Postkarten.**
(I would like)

- ☐ **das Eis** *(ice)*........................ ice cream ____________________
- ☐ **der Elefant** *(ay-lay-fahnt)*............ the elephant ____________________
- ☐ **das England** *(eng-lahnt)*............. England ____________________
  — where they speak **Englisch** ____________________
- ☐ **das Europa** *(oy-roh-pah)*............. Europe ____________________

(here) **Hier ist** a quick review of the *(fahr-ben)* **Farben.** Draw lines between **die** *(doych-en)* **deutschen Wörter** *(oont)* **und die** *(reehk-tee-gah)* **richtige** (correct) **Farbe.** On your mark, get set, *GO!*

(gelp) **gelb**	gray
(shvarts) **schwarz**	green
(grewn) **grün**	pink
(vice) **weiß**	multi-colored
(roht) **rot**	brown
(blau) **blau**	yellow
(boont) **bunt**	red
(roh-zah) **rosa**	black
(grau) **grau**	blue
(brown) **braun**	white

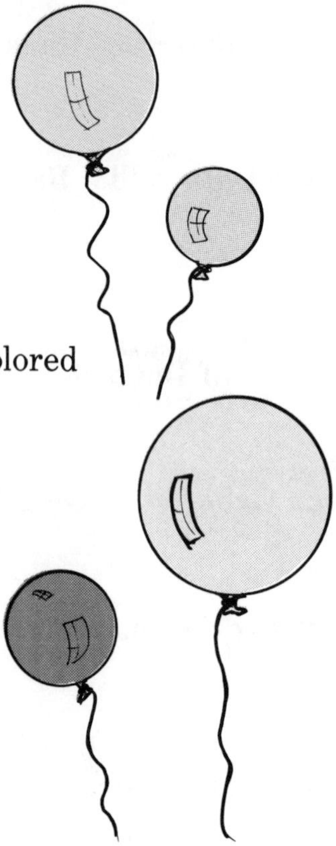

(noon) **Nun,** take a deep breath. Test your pronunciation on these *(doy-chah)* **deutsche** (German) proverbs.

(bore-gen) **Borgen** (borrowing) *(brinkt)* **bringt** (brings) *(zore-gen)* **Sorgen.** (sorrows)

(vee) **Wie** *(guh-vohn-en)* **gewonnen,** *(zoh)(tsair-rohn-en)* **so zerronnen!** (easy come, easy go)

(noon) **Nun,** (now) try these **deutsche** tongue-twisters. Are you ready?

(kly-nah) **Kleine** (small) *(kin-dair)* **Kinder** (children) *(kur-nen)* **können** (can't) *(kai-nah)* **keine** *(kirsh-kair-nah)* **Kirschkerne** *(knah-ken)* **knacken.** (crack cherry stones)

(kai-zairz) **Kaisers** (the Kaiser's) *(kurk-hen)* **Köchin** (cook) *(kahn)* **kann** (can't) *(kai-nen)* **keinen** *(kalps-kopf)* **Kalbskopf** *(kohk-hen)* **kochen.** (cook calf's head)

Don't worry if this seems difficult at first. Continue with the next Steps and come back to it later. You'll be surprised how quickly you improve — especially with practice!

- ☐ **europäisch** *(oy-roh-pay-ish)* .... European ________________
- ☐ **die Familie** *(fah-mee-lee-yah)* .... the family ________________
- ☐ **fantastisch** *(fahn-tahs-tish)* .... fantastic ________________
  — ex. **Das ist fantastisch!** ________________
- ☐ **der Februar** *(fay-broo-ahr)* .... February ________________

Step 6

(gelt)
das Geld
money

Before starting this Step, go back **und** review Step 4. Make sure you can count to *(tsvahn-tsig)* **zwanzig** without looking back at *(boohk)* **das Buch**. Let's learn the larger *(noo-mairn)* **Nummern** now, so if something costs more than 20 *(day-em)* **DM** you will know exactly *(vee-feel)* **wieviel** it costs. After practicing aloud *(dee)* **die deutschen Nummern** 10 through 100 below, write these *(noo-mairn)* **Nummern** in the blanks provided. Again, notice the similarities between numbers such as *(fewnf-tsig)* **fünfzig** (50), *(fewnf)* **fünf** (5) **und** *(fewnf-tsayn)* **fünfzehn** (15).

10	*(tsayn)* **zehn**	**(vier + sechs = zehn)**
20	*(tsvahn-tsig)* **zwanzig**	*(tsvai)* **(zwei = 2)**
30	*(dry-tsig)* **dreißig**	**(drei = 3)**
40	*(fear-tsig)* **vierzig**	**(vier = 4)**
50	*(fewnf-tsig)* **fünfzig**	**(fünf = 5)**
60	*(zex-tsig)* **sechzig**	**(sechs = 6)**
70	*(zeep-tsig)* **siebzig**	*(zee-ben)* **(sieben = 7)**
80	*(ahkt-tsig)* **achtzig**	**(acht = 8)**
90	*(noyn-tsig)* **neunzig**	**(neun = 9)**
100	*(hoon-dairt)* **hundert**	
1000	*(tau-zent)* **tausend**	

10 zehn ____________
20 ____________
30 ____________
40 ____________
50 ____________
60 ____________
70 ____________
80 ____________
90 ____________
100 ____________
1000 ____________

Now take a logical guess. *(vee)* **Wie** would you write **(und** say) the following? The answers *(zint)* **sind** at the bottom of the *(zigh-tah)* **Seite.**

400 ____________ 600 ____________

2000 ____________ 5300 ____________

ANTWORTEN

400 = vierhundert
2000 = zweitausend
600 = sechshundert
5300 = fünftausenddreihundert

The unit of currency **in Deutschland** *(doych-lahnt)* **ist die Deutsche Mark**, abbreviated **DM** *(day-em)*. Currency **ist** called **Scheine** *(shy-nah)* **und** coins are called **Kleingeld** *(kline-gelt)*. Just as **ein amerikanischer Dollar** *(ah-mair-ih-kahn-ish-air)(doh-lar)* can be broken down into 100 pennies, **eine** *(ine-ah)* **deutsche Mark** can be broken down into 100 **Pfennige** *(fen-ee-gah)*. A coin is called **ein Geldstück** *(gelt-shtewk)* (money piece) **und** you will also hear **Scheine** *(shy-nah)* (currency) referred to as **Geldscheine** *(gelt-shy-nah)*. Let's learn the various kinds of **Scheine** *(shy-nah)* (currency) **und Kleingeld** *(kline-gelt)* (coins). Always be sure to practice each **Wort** out loud. You might want to exchange some money **nun** *(noon)* (now) so that you can familiarize yourself **mit** the various **Kleingeld** *(kline-gelt)* (or **Geldstücken** *(gelt-shtewk-en)*) **und Scheine** (or **Geldscheinen** *(gelt-shy-nen)*).

ein Fünfmarkschein *(ine) (fewnf-mark-shine)* — a 5-mark bill

ein Zehnmarkschein *(tsayn-mark-shine)* — a 10-mark bill

ein Zwanzigmarkschein

ein Fünfzigmarkschein

ein Hundertmarkschein

ein Fünfhundertmarkschein

ein Tausendmarkschein

ein Einpfennigstück *(ine) (ine-fen-ig-shtewk)* — a 1-pfennig coin

ein Zweipfennigstück *(tsvai-fen-ig-shtewk)* — a 2-pfennig coin

ein Fünfpfennigstück *(fewnf-fen-ig-shtewk)* — a 5-pfennig coin

ein Zehnpfennigstück *(tsayn-fen-ig-shtewk)*

ein Fünfzigpfennigstück *(fewnf-tsig-fen-ig-shtewk)*

ein Markstück

ein Zweimarkstück *(tsvai-mark-shtewk)*

ein Fünfmarkstück *(fewnf-mark-shtewk)*

- ☐ **der Film** *(film)* . . . . film ____________
- ☐ **finden** *(fin-den)* . . . . to find ____________
  — ex. **Ich finde das Hotelzimmer.** ____________
- ☐ **der Finger** *(fing-air)* . . . . finger ____________
- ☐ **der Fisch** *(fish)* . . . . fish ____________

Review **die Nummern** *(tsayn)* **zehn** through *(tau-zent)* **tausend** again. *(noon)* **Nun,** how do you say "twenty-two" *(oh-dair)* **oder** "fifty-three" *(owf)* **auf Deutsch?** (in German) You basically talk backwards—*(zwei-und-zwanzig)* "two and twenty" **oder** *(drei-und-fünfzig)* "three and fifty." See if you can say **und** write out **die Nummern** on this *(zigh-tah)* **Seite.**

The answers *(zint)* **sind** at the bottom of the **Seite.**

a. 25 = ______________ (5 + 20)	b. 36 = ______________ (6 + 30)
c. 47 = siebenundvierzig (7 + 40)	d. 93 = ______________ (3 + 90)
e. 84 = ______________ (4 + 80)	f. 68 = ______________ (8 + 60)
g. 51 = ______________ (1 + 50)	h. 72 = ______________ (2 + 70)

To ask how much something costs *(owf)* **auf Deutsch,** one asks, *(vee-feel) (koh-stet) (dahs)* **„Wieviel kostet das?"** *(noon)* **Nun** (now) answer the following questions based on the *(noo-mairn)* **Nummern** (numbers) in parentheses.

1. *(vee-feel) (koh-stet)* **Wieviel kostet das?** (How much costs that?) **Es kostet** zehn (10) **Mark.**
2. **Wieviel kostet das?** **Es kostet** ______________ (20) **Mark.**
3. **Wieviel kostet das Buch?** **Es kostet** ______________ (17) **Mark.**
4. **Wieviel kostet das** *(ow-toh)* **Auto?** **Es kostet** ______________ (2000) **Mark.**
5. **Wieviel kostet** *(dair)* **der Film?** **Es kostet** ______________ (5) **Mark.**
6. **Wieviel kostet das** *(tsi-mair)* **Zimmer?** **Es kostet** ______________ (24) **Mark.**
7. **Wieviel kostet das** *(bilt)* **Bild?** **Es kostet** ______________ (923) **Mark.**

ANTWORTEN

a. **fünfundzwanzig**
b. **sechsunddreißig**
c. **siebenundvierzig**
d. **dreiundneunzig**
e. **vierundachtzig**
f. **achtundsechzig**
g. **einundfünfzig**
h. **zweiundsiebzig**

1. **zehn**
2. **zwanzig**
3. **siebzehn**
4. **zweitausend**
5. **fünf**
6. **vierundzwanzig**
7. **neunhundertdreiundzwanzig**

Congratulations!

Step 7

(hoy-tah) **Heute,** today *(more-gen)* **morgen,** tomorrow *(oont)* **und** and *(ges-tairn)* **gestern** yesterday

der Kalender
(kah-len-dair)

Eine Woche hat sieben Tage.
(voh-kah) Woche = week; *(haht)* hat; *(tah-gah)* Tage = days

(zohn-tahk) **Sonntag**	*(mohn-tahk)* **Montag**	*(deens-tahk)* **Dienstag**	*(mit-vohk)* **Mittwoch**	*(doh-nairs-tahk)* **Donnerstag**	*(fry-tahk)* **Freitag**	*(zahms-tahk)* **Samstag**
1	2	3	4	5	6	7

Es ist *(zair)* **sehr** (very) important to know the days of the week **und** the various parts of the *(tahk)* **Tag** (day). Let's learn them. Be sure to say them aloud before filling in the blanks below.

(zohn-tahk) **Sonntag** ____________	*(mohn-tahk)* **Montag** Montag
(deens-tahk) **Dienstag** ____________	*(mit-vohk)* **Mittwoch** ____________
(doh-nairs-tahk) **Donnerstag** ____________	*(fry-tahk)* **Freitag** ____________
(zahms-tahk) **Samstag** ____________	

If *(hoy-tah)* **heute ist Mittwoch**, then *(more-gen)* **morgen ist Donnerstag und** *(ges-tairn)* **gestern** *(vahr)* **war** (was) **Dienstag**. *(noon)* **Nun,** you supply the correct answers. If **heute ist Montag**, then **morgen ist** ____________ **und gestern war** ____________. Or, if **heute ist Montag**, then morgen **ist Dienstag und** ____________ **war Sonntag. Was ist heute? Heute ist** ____________.

(noon) **Nun,** peel off the next *(zee-ben)* **sieben** labels *(oont)* **und** put them on a *(kah-len-dair)* **Kalender** you use every *(tahk)* **Tag** (day).

From **nun** on—Monday **ist „Montag!"**

- ☐ **frei** *(fry)* .... free, no charge, available ____________
- ☐ **der Garten** *(gar-ten)* .... garden ____________
- ☐ **das Glas** *(glahs)* .... glass ____________
- ☐ **gut** *(goot)* .... good ____________
  — ex. **nicht gut** = not good ____________

There are **vier** *(fear)* parts to each **Tag** *(tahk)* [day].

morning	= **der Morgen** *(more-gen)*	der Morgen
afternoon	= **der Nachmittag** *(nahk-mit-tahk)*	
evening	= **der Abend** *(ah-bent)*	
night	= **die Nacht** *(nahkt)*	

Notice that **morgen** means "tomorrow" **und der Morgen** means "morning" **auf Deutsch.**

Nun, fill in the following blanks **und** then check your **Antworten** *(ahnt-vor-ten)* at the bottom of the **Seite** *(zigh-táh)* [page].

a.	Sunday morning	=	Sonntag morgen
b.	Friday evening	=	
c.	Saturday evening	=	
d.	Monday morning	=	
e.	Wednesday morning	=	
f.	Tuesday afternoon	=	
g.	Thursday afternoon	=	
h.	Thursday night	=	
i.	yesterday evening	=	
j.	this afternoon (today)	=	heute nachmittag
k.	this morning	=	
l.	tomorrow afternoon	=	
m.	tomorrow evening	=	

ANTWORTEN

a. **Sonntag morgen**
b. **Freitag abend**
c. **Samstag abend**
d. **Montag morgen**
e. **Mittwoch morgen**
f. **Dienstag nachmittag**
g. **Donnerstag nachmittag**
h. **Donnerstag nacht**
i. **gestern abend**
j. **heute nachmittag**
k. **heute morgen**
l. **morgen nachmittag**
m. **morgen abend**

So **mit** merely **elf** *(vur-tair)* **Wörter** you can specify any day of the *(voh-kah)* **Woche und** any time of the *(tahk)* **Tag.** (mit = with; Woche = week)

Die Wörter *(hoy-tah)* **heute**, *(more-gen)* **morgen**, **und** *(ges-tairn)* **gestern** will be *(zair)* **sehr** important for you in making reservations *(oont)* **und** appointments, in getting *(tay-ah-tair-kar-ten)* **Theaterkarten und** many things you will wish to do. Knowing the parts of the *(tahk)* **Tag** will help you to learn **und** understand the various *(doy-chah)* **deutsche** greetings below. Practice these every *(tahk)* **Tag nun** until your trip.

good morning	=	*(goo-ten) (more-gen)* **Guten Morgen**	
good day (hello)	=	*(goo-ten) (tahk)* **Guten Tag**	
good evening	=	*(goo-ten) (ah-bent)* **Guten Abend**	Guten Abend
good night	=	*(goo-tah) (nahkt)* **Gute Nacht**	
How are you?	=	*(vee) (gate) (ee-nen)* **Wie geht es Ihnen?**	

Take the next *(fear)* **vier** labels *(oont)* **und** stick them on the appropriate *(ding-ah)* **Dinge** (things) in your *(house)* **Haus.** *(vee)* **Wie** about the bathroom mirror *(fewr)* **für Guten Morgen?** *(oh-dair)* **Oder** the front door **für Guten Abend?** *(oh-dair)* **Oder** your alarm clock *(fewr)* **für** (for) **Gute Nacht? Oder** your kitchen cabinet **für Guten Tag?** Remember that, whenever you enter shops **und** stores **in** *(doych-lahnt)* **Deutschland,** you will hear the appropriate greeting for the time of day. Don't be surprised. **Es ist** a *(zair)* **sehr** (very) friendly custom. Everyone greets everyone *(oont)* **und** you should too, if you really want to enjoy *(doych-lahnt)* **Deutschland!** You *(zint)* **sind** about one-fourth of your way through **das** *(boohk)* **Buch und es ist** a good time to quickly review **die** *(vur-tair)* **Wörter** you *(hah-ben)* **haben** learned before doing the crossword puzzle on the next *(zigh-tah)* **Seite.** *(feel)* **Viel** *(shpahss)* **Spaß und** *(feel)* **viel** *(glewk)* **Glück!** *(oh-dair)* **Oder,** as we say *(owf)* **auf Englisch,** much fun and lots of luck!

ANTWORTEN TO CROSSWORD PUZZLE

ACROSS

1. Dienstag
2. Nachmittag
3. Mittwoch
4. heute
5. Donnerstag
6. fünf
7. Abend
8. dreißig
9. wieviel
10. Amerika
11. sieben
12. frei
13. Bank
14. gestern
15. Wein
16. blau
17. der/die/das
18. sechzig
19. rosa
20. haben
21. Tag
22. vier
23. gelb
24. zwanzig
25. gut
26. warum
27. Büro
28. Bier
29. in

DOWN

1. neun
2. Sonntag
3. Auto
4. Nacht
5. Familie
6. morgen
7. Montag
8. Samstag
9. weiß
10. wer
11. elf
12. Freitag
13. Bus
14. kommen
15. Mark
16. bunt
17. Bild
18. eins
19. rot
20. Tee
21. Bett
22. vierzig
23. grau
24. Zug
25. grün
26. wo
27. in
28. schwarz

(kroits-vort-rate-sel)
DAS KREUZWORTRÄTSEL

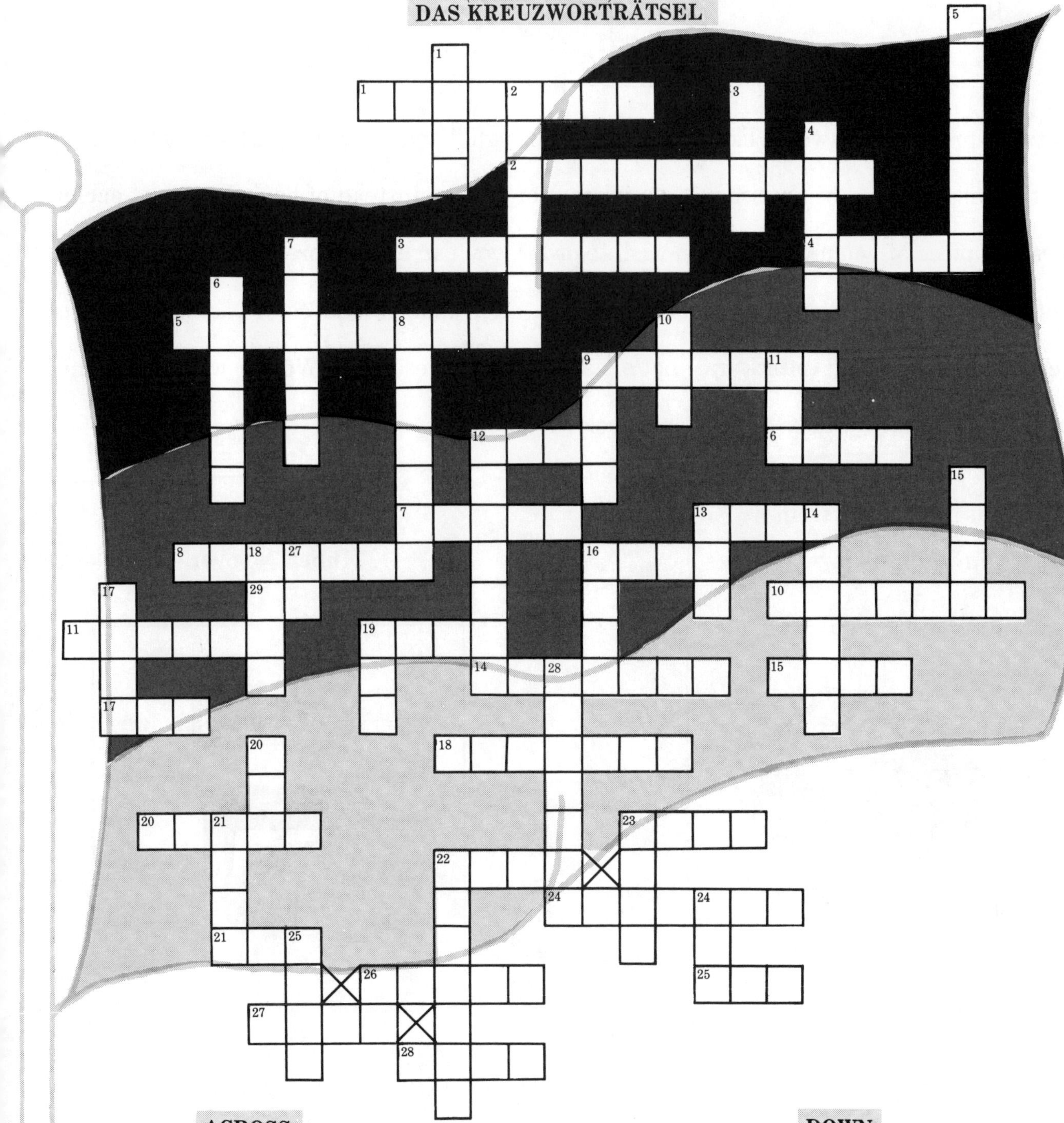

ACROSS

1. Tuesday
2. afternoon
3. Wednesday
4. today
5. Thursday
6. 5
7. evening
8. 30
9. how much
10. America
11. 7
12. free
13. bank
14. yesterday
15. wine
16. blue
17. the (many possibilities)
18. 60
19. pink
20. to have
21. day
22. 4
23. yellow
24. 20
25. good
26. why
27. office
28. beer
29. into

DOWN

1. 9
2. Sunday
3. car
4. night
5. family
6. tomorrow/morning
7. Monday
8. Saturday
9. white
10. who
11. 11
12. Friday
13. bus
14. to come
15. unit of **Deutsche** currency
16. multi-colored
17. picture
18. 1
19. red
20. tea
21. bed
22. 40
23. gray
24. train
25. green
26. where
27. in
28. black

Step 8

(in) (on) (owf)
In, an, auf . .
in on on top of

(doy-chah) (zint)
Deutsche prepositions (words like "in," "on," "through," and "next to") **sind** easy to learn (oont) **und** they allow you to be precise **mit** a minimum of effort. Instead of having to point (zex) **sechs** times at a piece of yummy pastry you wish to order, you can explain precisely which one you want by saying **es ist** behind, in front of, next to, (oh-dair) **oder** under the piece of pastry which the salesperson **ist** starting to pick up. Let's learn some of these little (vur-tair) **Wörter** which are (zair) **sehr** similar to (eng-leash) **Englisch.** Study the examples below.

(ows) **aus** = out of / from
in = into / in
(nay-ben) **neben** = next to
(oon-tair) **unter** = under
(ew-bair) **über** = over

(dair) (mahn) (gate) (noy-ah)
Der Mann geht in das neue Hotel.
goes

(dee) (frow) (kohmt) (ows) (daim) (goo-ten)
Die Frau kommt aus dem guten Hotel.
comes

(arts-t) (daim)
Der Arzt ist in dem guten Hotel.
doctor

(noy-ah) (bilt) (daim)
Das neue Bild ist über dem Tisch.

Das neue Bild ist neben der Uhr.

Der braune Tisch ist unter dem Bild.

(grau-ah) (hoont)
Der graue Hund ist neben dem Tisch.

(grewn-ah)
Die grüne Uhr ist über dem Tisch.

Die grüne Uhr ist neben dem Bild.

☐ **ich** *(eehk)*. I
☐ **die Information** *(in-for-mah-tsee-ohn)*. . . information
— also known as **Auskunft**
☐ **interessant** *(in-tair-es-sahnt)*. . . . . interesting
— ex. **Das ist sehr interessant.**

Fill in the blanks below **mit** the correct prepositions according to the *(bil-dair)* **Bilder** (pictures) on the previous *(zigh-tah)* **Seite.**

Der *(mahn)* **Mann** *(gate)* **geht** in **das neue Hotel.**

Der *(grau-ah)* **graue Hund ist** ________ **dem Tisch.**

Die grüne Uhr ist ________ *(daim)* **dem Tisch.**

Der *(arts-t)* **Arzt ist** ________ *(daim)* **dem guten Hotel.**

Die *(grewn-ah)* **grüne Uhr ist** ________ **dem Bild.**

Das *(noy-ah)* **neue Bild ist** ________ **dem Tisch.**

Der braune Tisch ist ________ **dem Bild.**

Das neue Bild ist ________ **der Uhr.**

Die *(frow)* **Frau kommt** ________ **dem guten Hotel.**

(noon) **Nun,** answer these questions based on the *(bil-dair)* **Bilder** on the previous *(zigh-tah)* **Seite.**

(voh) **Wo ist der** *(arts-t)* **Arzt?** ________________________________

Wo ist der *(hoont)* **Hund?** ________________________________

Wo ist der Tisch? ________________________________

Wo ist das Bild? ________________________________

(vahs) **Was** *(mahkt)* **macht** (does) *(dee)* **die Frau?** ________________________________

Was *(mahkt)* **macht** (does) **der Mann?** ________________________________

Ist die Uhr *(grewn)* **grün?** Ja, die Uhr ist grün.

Ist der Hund *(grau)* **grau?** Ja,

- ☐ **das Institut** *(in-stee-toot)* .... institution ________
- ☐ **das Italien** *(ee-tah-lee-en)* .... Italy ________
  —where they speak **Italienisch** *(ee-tah-lee-ay-nish)* ________
- ☐ **ja** *(yah)* .... yes ________
- ☐ **die Jacke** *(yah-kah)* .... jacket ________

Nun *(noon)* for some more practice **mit deutschen** prepositions!

auf *(owf)* = on top of (horizontal surfaces)

an *(on)* = on/upon (vertical surfaces)

vor *(for)* = in front of

hinter *(hin-tair)* = behind

Das *(dahs)* **Glas Wasser** *(vah-sair)* **ist auf** *(owf)* **dem** *(daim)* **Tisch.**	**Das Glas Wasser ist _____ dem Tisch.**
Das bunte *(boon-tah)* **Bild ist an** *(on)* **der Wand** *(vahnt)*.	**Das bunte Bild ist** an **der Wand.**
Die gelbe *(gel-bah)* **Lampe ist hinter** *(hin-tair)* **dem Tisch.**	**Die gelbe Lampe ist _____ dem Tisch.**
Der braune Tisch ist vor *(for)* **dem Bett.**	**Der braune Tisch ist _____ dem Bett.**
Das bunte *(boon-tah)* **Bett ist hinter dem braunen Tisch.**	**Das bunte Bett ist _____ dem braunen Tisch.**

Answer the following **Fragen** *(frah-gen)* (questions), based on the **Bilder** *(bil-dair)*, by filling in the blanks **mit** the correct prepositions. Choose the prepositions from those you **haben** *(hah-ben)* just learned.

Wo *(voh)* **ist das rote** *(roh-tah)* **Buch** *(boohk)*?

Das rote Buch *(boohk)* **ist _____ dem braunen Tisch.**

Wo ist der blaue Bus *(boos)*?

Der blaue Bus ist _____ dem grauen Hotel.

- ☐ **das Jahr** *(yahr)*. . . . . year _______________
- ☐ **der Januar** *(yah-noo-ar)*. . . . . January _______________
- ☐ **das Japan** *(ya-pahn)*. . . . . Japan _______________
  — where they speak **Japanisch** *(ya-pahn-ish)* _______________
- ☐ **das Journal** *(zhur-nahl)*. . . . . magazine _______________

Wo *(voh)* **ist das graue Telefon** *(tay-lay-fohn)*? **Wo ist der grüne** *(grewn-ah)* **Teppich** *(tep-eeh)*? **Wo ist das Bild?**

Das *(dahs)* **graue Telefon ist** ____________ **der weißen** *(vice-en)* **Wand** *(vahnt)*.

Das graue Telefon ist ____________ **dem** *(daim)* **bunten** *(boon-ten)* **Bild.**

Das graue Telefon ist __________ **dem schwarzen** *(shvar-tsen)* **Tisch.**

Der grüne Teppich ist __________ **dem schwarzen Tisch.**

Das Bild ist ___an___ **der weißen** *(vice-en)* **Wand** *(vahnt)*.

Nun fill in each blank on the **Hotel** below **mit** the best possible preposition. The correct **Antworten** *(ahnt-vor-ten)* **sind** at the bottom of the **Seite. Viel** *(feel)* **Spaß.**

1. ____________

2. ____________

3. ____________

4. ____________

5. ____________

6. ___in___

7. ____________

8. ____________

9. ____________

10. ____________

ANTWORTEN

1. **über**	3. **hinter**	5. **in**	7. **neben**	9. **unter**
2. **auf**	4. **an**	6. **in**	8. **vor**	10. **aus**

Step 9

Januar *(jah-noo-ar)*, Februar *(fay-broo-ar)*, März *(merts)*

Dreißig Tage hat *(haht)* [has] **September** *(zep-tem-bair)*, **April** *(ah-pril)*, **Juni** *(you-nee)*, **und November** *(noh-vem-bair)* **. . .**

Sound familiar? You **haben** *(hah-ben)* learned the days of the **Woche** *(voh-kah)*, so now **es ist** time to learn **die Monate** *(moh-nah-tah)* [months] of the **Jahr** *(yahr)* [year] **und** all the different kinds of **Wetter** *(vet-tair)* [weather] which you might encounter on your holiday. For example, you ask about **das Wetter** *(vet-tair)* **auf Deutsch** just as you would **auf Englisch**—**„Wie** *(vee)* [how] **ist** [is] **das** [the] **Wetter** [weather] **heute?“** *(hoy-tah)* [today] Practice all the possible answers to this **Frage** *(frah-gah)* [question] **und dann** *(don)* [then] write the following answers in the blanks below.

Wie *(vee)* ist das Wetter heute *(hoy-tah)*?

Es regnet *(rayg-net)* [rains] **heute.** ______________________________

Es schneit *(shnait)* [snows] **heute.** ______________________________

Es ist warm *(varm)* [warm] **heute.** ______________________________

Es ist kalt *(kahlt)* [cold] **heute.** Es ist kalt heute.

Es ist schön *(shurn)* [pretty] **heute.** ______________________________

Es ist schlecht *(shleckt)* [bad] **heute.** ______________________________

Es ist heiß *(hice)* [hot] **heute.** ______________________________

Es ist neblig *(nay-blig)* [foggy] **heute.** ______________________________

Nun practice the **Wörter** on the next **Seite** aloud **und dann** *(don)* [then] fill in the blanks **mit** the names of the month **und** the appropriate weather report.

- ☐ **der Juli** *(you-lee)*. . . . . July ______________
- ☐ **der Juni** *(you-nee)*. . . . . June ______________

— Mit den freien K Wörtern, notice how often **Englisch** "c" becomes "k" **auf Deutsch.**

- ☐ **der Kaffee** *(kah-fay)*. . . . . coffee ______________
- ☐ **das Kaffeehaus** *(kah-fay-house)*. . . . . . . coffee house ______________

im (im) [in] Januar (jah-noo-ar) ________ Es schneit (shnait) im Januar. ________

im Februar (fay-broo-ar) ________ Es schneit auch (owk) [also] im Februar. ________

im März (merts) ________ Es regnet (rayg-net) im März. Es regnet im März.

im April (ah-pril) ________ Es regnet auch im April. ________

im Mai (my) ________ Es ist windig (vin-dig) [windy] im Mai. ________

im Juni (you-nee) ________ Es ist auch windig im Juni. ________

im Juli (you-lee) im Juli Es ist warm (varm) im Juli. ________

im August (ow-goost) ________ Es ist heiß (hice) im August. ________

im September (zep-tem-bair) ________ Es ist schön (shurn) im September. ________

im Oktober (ohk-toh-bair) ________ Es ist neblig (nay-blig) im Oktober. ________

im November (noh-vem-bair) ________ Es ist kalt (kahlt) im November. ________

im Dezember (day-tsem-bair) ________ Es ist schlecht (shleckt) im Dezember. ________

Nun answer the following **Fragen** (frah-gen) based on the **Bilder** (bil-dair) to the right.

Wie ist das Wetter (vet-tair) **im** [in] **Februar** (fay-broo-ar)**?** ________

Wie ist das Wetter im April (ah-pril)**?** ________

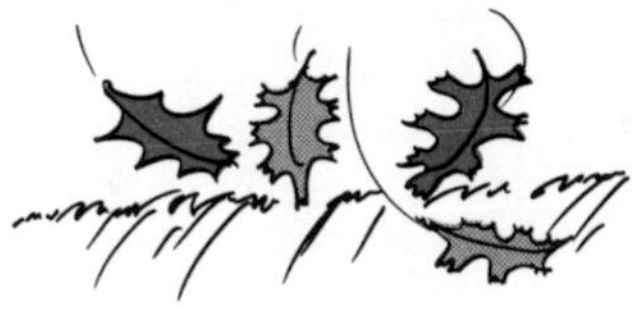

Wie ist das Wetter im Mai (my)**?** ________

Wie ist das Wetter im August (ow-goost)**?** ________

Ist das Wetter heute (hoy-tah) [today] **gut oder schlecht?** ________

- ☐ **der Kakao** *(ka-kow)* .... hot chocolate ________
- ☐ **kalt** *(kahlt)* .... cold ________
- ☐ **die Karotten** *(kah-roh-ten)* .... carrots ________
- ☐ **die Karten** *(kar-ten)* .... cards ________
- ☐ **kommen** *((koh-men)* .... to come ________

(fewr) (yahr)
Nun für the seasons of the **Jahr** . . .
year

(vin-tair) **der Winter**	(zoh-mair) **der Sommer**	(hairp-st) **der Herbst** autumn	(frew-ling) **der Frühling** spring

der Winter	____________	____________	____________
(kahlt) **Es ist kalt im Winter.** (im = in)	(hice) **Es ist heiß im Sommer.**	(vin-dig) **Es ist windig im Herbst.**	(rayg-net) **Es regnet im Frühling.**

At this point **es ist eine** (goo-tah) **gute** [good] (ee-day) **Idee** [idea] to familiarize yourself **mit** (oy-roh-pay-ish-en) **europäischen** [European] (tem-pair-ah-toor-en) **Temperaturen** [temperatures]. Carefully read the typical weather forecasts below **und** study the thermometer because temperatures **in** (oy-roh-pah) **Europa** are calculated on the basis of Centigrade (not Fahrenheit).

(fah-ren-hait) **Fahrenheit**	(sell-see-oos) **Celsius** Centigrade	
212° F	100° C	(vah-sair) **Wasser kocht** [boils]
98.6° F	37° C	(nor-mah-lah) **Normale** [normal] **Bluttemperatur** [blood temperature]
68° F	20° C	
32° F	0° C	(zeus-vah-sair) **Süßwasser friert** [fresh water freezes]
0° F	-17.8° C	(zahlts-vah-sair) **Salzwasser friert** [salt water freezes]
-10° F	-23.3° C	

Das (vet-tair) **Wetter** (fewr) **für Montag,** (dain) **den 21.** (merts) **März:**

> **kalt und windig**
> (tem-pair-ah-toor) **Temperatur:** 5 (graht) **Grad** [degrees]

Das Wetter für Dienstag, den 18. Juli:

> **warm und schön**
> **Temperatur: 20 Grad**

- ☐ **der Kilometer** *(kee-loh-may-tair)*....... kilometer ____________
  — A **Kilometer ist** 1000 meters. ____________
- ☐ **kochen** *(kohk-hen)*.................. to cook ____________
  — ex. **Ich koche in der Küche.** ____________
- ☐ **das Konzert** *(kohn-tsairt)*............ concert ____________

(kin-dair) Kinder, *(kew-sha)* Küche, und *(kirh-ha)* Kirche
children, kitchen, church

Just as we have the "3 R's" *(owf)* **auf Englisch, auf Deutsch** there are the "3 K's."

Kinder  **K**üche  **K**irche 

Study **das** *(bilt)* **Bild** below *(oont)* **und** *(don)* **dann** write out **die** *(noy-en)* **neuen** *(vur-tair)* **Wörter** in the blanks on the next **Seite.**

(stahm-baum)
der Stammbaum
family tree

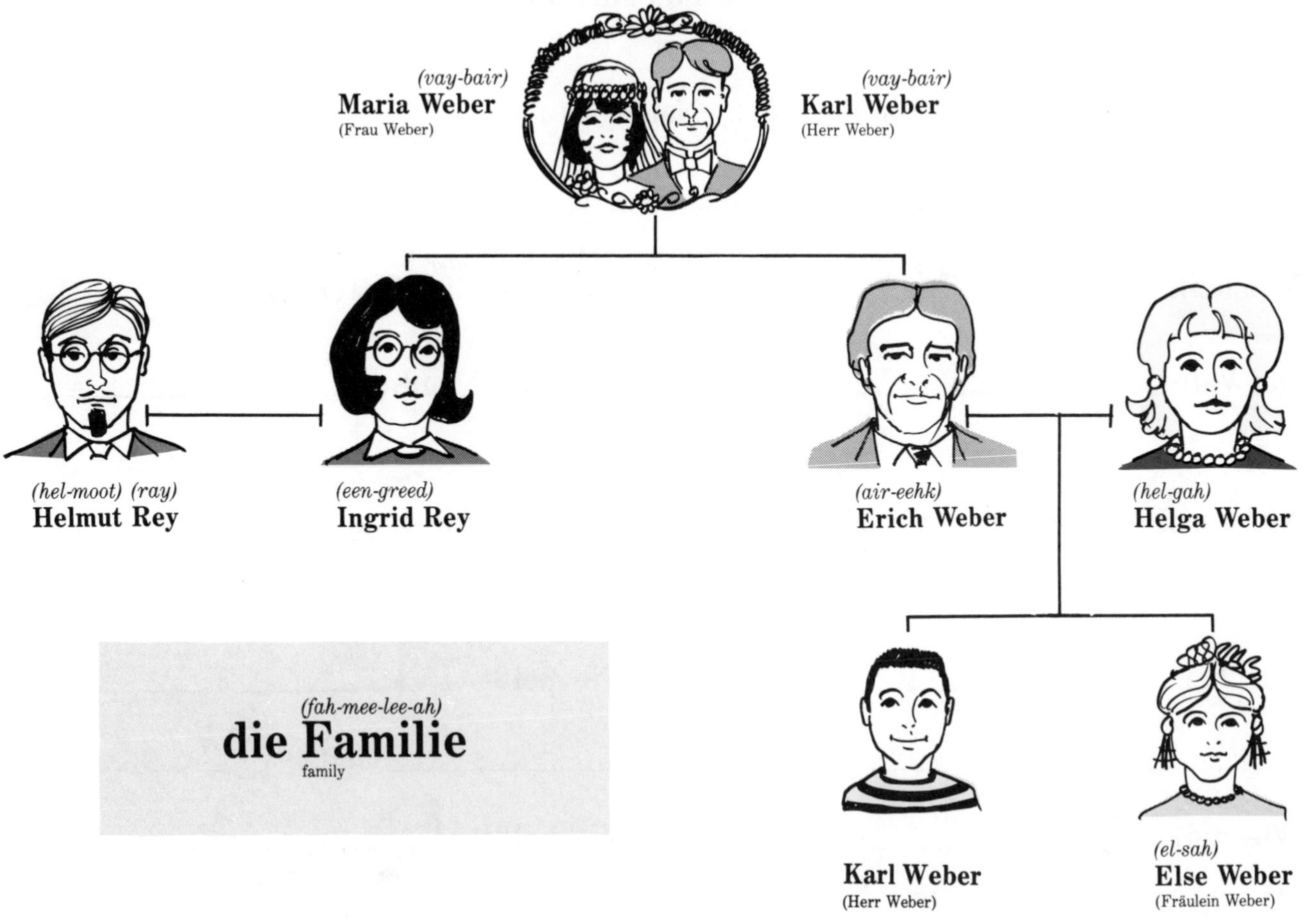

(fah-mee-lee-ah)
die Familie
family

- ☐ **kosten** *(koh-sten)* .... to cost ______________
  — ex. **Es kostet 10 Mark.** ______________
- ☐ **das Kotelett** *(koh-te-let)* .... cutlet ______________
- ☐ **kühl** *(kewl)* .... cool ______________
- ☐ **der Kühlschrank** *(kewl-shrahnk)* ...... cool closet/refrigerator ______________

die Großeltern *(grohs-el-tairn)* — grandparents

 **die Eltern** *(el-tairn)* — parents 

der Großvater *(grohs-fah-tair)* — grandfather: der Großvater
die Großmutter *(grohs-moo-tair)* — grandmother: ____________

der Vater *(fah-tair)* — father: ____________
die Mutter *(moo-tair)* — mother: ____________

 **die Kinder** *(kin-dair)* — children 

der Sohn *(zohn)* — son: ____________
die Tochter *(tohk-tair)* — daughter: ____________

 **die Verwandten** *(fair-vahn-ten)* — relatives 

der Onkel *(ohn-kel)* — uncle: ____________
die Tante *(tahn-tah)* — aunt: ____________

Der Sohn und die Tochter sind auch Bruder *(broo-dair)* brother und Schwester *(shves-tair)* sister!

Let's learn how to identify **die Familie** *(fah-mee-lee-ah)* family by **Name** *(nah-mah)* name. Study the following examples.

Wie how **heißt** *(heist)* is called **der** *(dair)* the **Vater?** father 

Der Vater heißt is called Erich.

Wie heißt *(heist)* is called **die** *(dee)* **Mutter?** 

Die Mutter heißt is called Helga.

Nun you fill in the following blanks, based on the **Bilder,** in the same manner.

Wie heißt  der Sohn?

____________ **heißt** ____________.

Wie heißt  ____________?

____________ **heißt** Else.

Wie heißt  ____________?

____________ **heißt** ____________.

Wie heißt  ____________?

____________ **heißt** ____________.

- ☐ **landen** *(lahn-den)*.................... to land ____________
- ☐ **das Lamm** *(lahm)*.................... lamb ____________
- ☐ **die Lampe** *(lahm-pah)*............... lamp ____________
- ☐ **das Land** *(lahnt)*.................... land/country ____________
- ☐ **die Landmarke** *(lahnt-mar-kah)*....... landmark ____________

(kew-sha)
die Küche
kitchen

Study all these (bil-dair) **Bilder und** (don) **dann** practice saying **und** writing out **die Wörter**.

Das ist die (kew-sha) **Küche.**

(dair) (kewl-shrahnk)
der Kühlschrank

der Kühlschrank

(oh-fen) (hairt)
der Ofen / der Herd

(vine)
der Wein

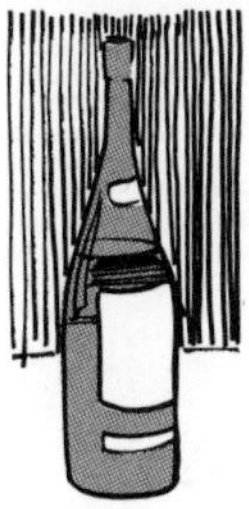

(beer)
das Bier

(milsh)
die Milch

(boo-tair)
die Butter

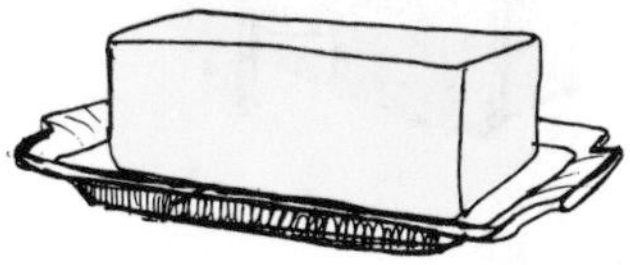

Answer these questions aloud.

(voh)
Wo ist das Bier? .... Das Bier ist in dem Kühlschrank.

Wo ist *(dee)* **die Milch?** **Wo ist der Wein?** **Wo ist die Butter?**

☐ **die Landung** *(lahn-doong)*............ landing
☐ **lang** *(lahng)*......................... long (vs. short = **kurz**)
☐ **laut** *(lout)*.......................... loud (vs. soft = **leise**)
☐ **lernen** *(lair-nen)*.................... to learn
☐ **das Licht** *(leeht)*.................... light

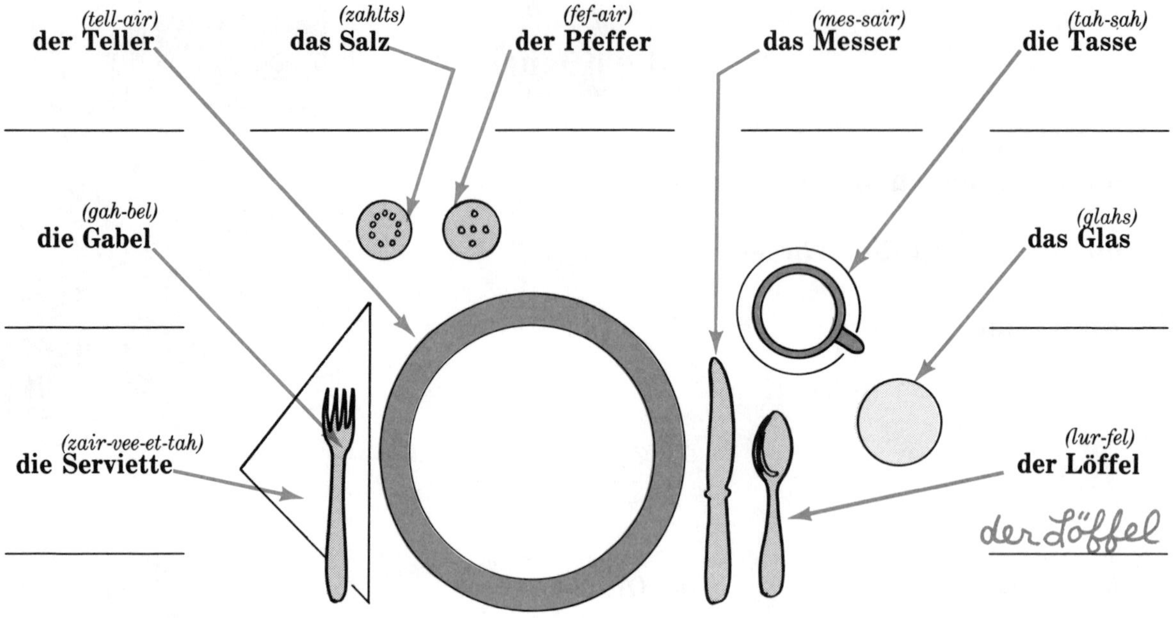

(oont) (mair)
Und mehr . . .
more

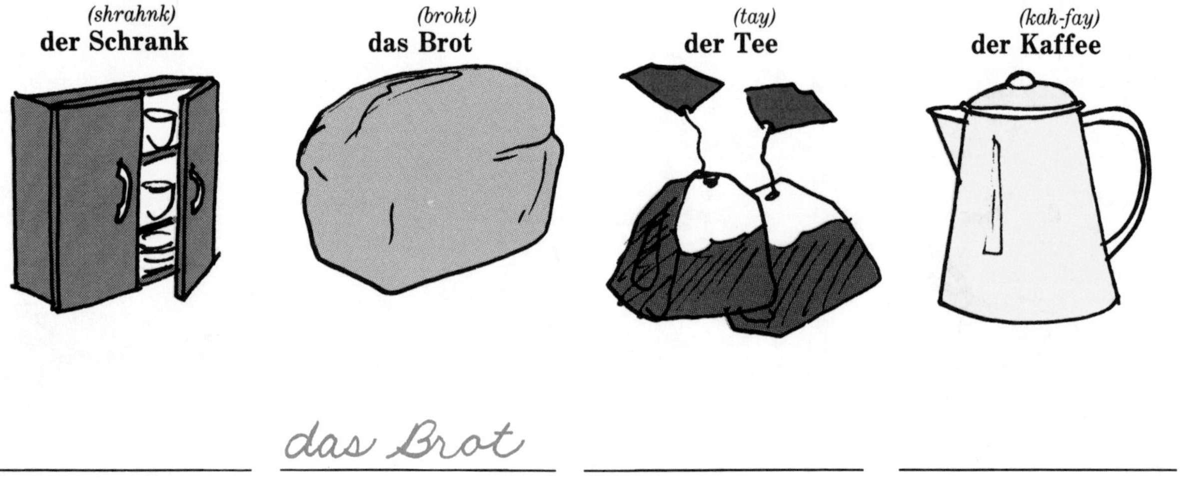

Wo *(voh)* **ist das Brot? Das Brot ist in dem Schrank** *(shrahnk)*. **Wo ist der Tee** *(tay)*? **Wo ist der Kaffee** *(kah-fay)*?

Nun öffnen *(urf-nen)* (open) your **Buch** *(boohk)* to the **Seite** *(zigh-tah)* **mit** the labels **und** remove the next **neunzehn** *(noyn-tsayn)* labels **und** proceed to label all these **Dinge** in your **Küche** *(kew-sha)*. Do not forget to use every opportunity to say these **Wörter** out loud. **Das ist sehr** *(zair)* **wichtig** *(veehk-teeg)* (important).

☐ **der Likör** *(lee-kur)*.................. liqueur ____________________
☐ **die Limonade** *(lee-moh-nah-dah)*...... lemonade ____________________
☐ **die Linie** *(lee-nee-ah)*................ line ____________________
☐ **die Lokomotive** *(loh-koh-moh-tee-vah)*.. locomotive ____________________
☐ **das Luxemburg** *(loox-em-boorg)*....... Luxembourg ____________________

(kirh-ha) **die Kirche** (church)

In Deutschland, there **ist** not the wide variety of **Religionen** *(ray-lee-gee-ohn-en)* (religions) that **wir** *(vir)* (we) **finden** *(fin-den)* (find) **hier in Amerika**. A person's **Religion** *(ray-lee-gee-ohn)* **ist** usually one of the following.

1. **evangelisch** *(eh-vahn-gay-lish)* (Protestant) evangelisch ____________
2. **katholisch** *(kah-toh-lish)* (Catholic) ____________
3. **jüdisch** *(yew-dish)* (Jewish) ____________

Hier ist eine Kirche *(kirh-ha)* **in Deutschland** *(doych-lahnt)***.** **Ist das eine katholische** *(kah-toh-lish-ah)* **oder evangelische** *(ay-vahn-gay-lish-ah)* **Kirche? Ist das eine neue** *(noy-ah)* **Kirche? Nein,** *(nine)* **das ist eine sehr alte** *(ahl-tah)* (old) **Kirche.** You will see **viele** *(feel-ah)* (many) **schöne** *(shurn-ah)* (pretty) **Kirchen** *(kirh-hen)* like this during your holiday **in Deutschland.**

Nun let's learn how to say "I am" **auf Deutsch**: I am = **ich** *(eehk)* **bin** ____________

Practice saying **„ich bin" mit** the following **Wörtern** *(vur-tairn)***. Nun** write each sentence for more practice.

Ich bin katholisch. ____________ **Ich bin evangelisch.** ____________

Ich bin jüdisch. Ich bin jüdisch. ____________ **Ich bin Amerikaner** *(ah-mair-ih-kahn-air)***.** ____________

Ich bin in Europa *(oy-roh-pah)***.** ____________ **Ich bin in Deutschland.** ____________

- ☐ **der Mai** *(my)*. . . . . May ____________
- ☐ **der Mann** *(mahn)*. . . . . man ____________
- ☐ **der Markt** *(markt)* . . . . market ____________
  — usually an open-air market in the town square ____________
- ☐ **die Marmelade** *(mahr-mih-lah-dah)*. . . . marmalade ____________

Ich bin in der *(kirh-ha)* **Kirche.** ______________ Ich bin in der *(kew-sha)* **Küche.** ______________

Ich bin die *(moo-tair)* **Mutter.** Ich bin die Mutter. Ich bin der *(fah-tair)* **Vater.** ______________

Ich bin in *(daim)* **dem Hotel.** ______________ Ich bin in dem Restaurant. ______________

Ich bin *(hoon-grig)* **hungrig.** (hungry) ______________ Ich bin *(dur-stig)* **durstig.** (thirsty) ______________

Nun identify all **die** *(pair-zoh-nen)* **Personen** (people) **in dem Bild** below by writing **das** *(reeh-tee-gah)* **richtige** (correct) **deutsche Wort** for each person on the line with the corresponding number *(oon-tair)* **unter dem Bild.**

1. ______________ 2. ______________

3. ______________ 4. ______________

5. der Onkel 6. ______________

7. ______________

☐ **der Mechaniker** *(may-kahn-ee-kair)*.... mechanic ______________
☐ **die Meile** *(my-lah)*.................. mile ______________
— 1 mile = 1.67 **Kilometer** ______________
☐ **der Meter** *(may-tair)*................ meter ______________
— Ein Meter ist about 1 yard; a **Kilometer ist** 1000 **Meter**. ______________

(lair-nen)
Lernen!
learn

You **haben** already used the verbs **haben** *(hah-ben)* **und möchten** *(murk-ten)*, **kosten** *(koh-sten)* (to cost), **finden, kochen** *(kohk-hen)* (to cook), **kommen** *(koh-men)*, **gehen, ist, sind, und bin.** Although you might be able to "get by" **mit** these verbs, let's assume you want to do **besser** *(bess-air)* (better) than that. First a quick review.

How do you say "I" **auf Deutsch?** ich How do you say "we" **auf Deutsch?** ____

Compare these **zwei** *(tsvai)* charts **sehr** carefully **und** learn these **sieben Wörter** on the right.

I	=	**ich** *(eehk)*
he	=	**er** *(air)*
she	=	**sie** *(zee)*
it	=	**es** *(es)*

we	=	**wir** *(vir)*
you	=	**Sie** *(zee)*
they	=	**sie** *(zee)*

Nun draw lines between the matching **englische und deutsche Wörter** *(vur-tair)* below to see if you can keep these **Wörter** straight in your mind.

wir	I
es	you
er	he
sie	we
ich	she
Sie	it
sie	they

Nun close **das Buch und** write out both columns of the above practice on **ein Stück** *(shtewk)* **Papier** *(pah-peer)*. How did **Sie** do? **Gut** *(goot)* **oder schlecht?** *(shleckt)* (bad) **Gut** *(goot)* **oder nicht so** *(zoh)* **gut? Nun** that **Sie** know these **Wörter, Sie** can say almost anything **auf Deutsch** with one basic formula: the "plug-in" formula. With this formula, you can correctly use any **Wörter Sie** wish.

- ☐ **mehr** *(mair)* . . . . more ________
- ☐ **die Milch** *(milsh)* . . . . milk ________
- ☐ **die Mitte** *(mit-tah)* . . . . middle ________
- ☐ **der Montag** *(mohn-tahk)* . . . . Monday ________
- ☐ **der Morgen** *(more-gen)* . . . . morning ________

To demonstrate, let's take *(zex)* **sechs** basic **und** practical verbs **und** see how the "plug-in" formula works. Write **die Verben** (verbs) in the blanks below after **Sie haben** practiced saying them.

(koh-men) **kommen** = to come	*(gay-en)* **gehen** = to go	*(lair-nen)* **lernen** = to learn
kommen	______________	______________
(brow-ken) **brauchen** = to need	*(hah-ben)* **haben** = to have	*(murk-ten)* **möchten** = would like
______________	______________	______________

Study the following verb patterns carefully.

(eehk) **ich**	*(koh-mah)* **komme**	= I *come*
	(gay-ah) **gehe**	= I *go*
	(lair-nah) **lerne**	= I *learn*
	(brow-kah) **brauche**	= I *need*
	(hah-bah) **habe**	= I *have*
	(murk-tah) **möchte**	= I *would like*

(air) **er**, *(zee)* **sie**, *(es)* **es**	*(kohmt)* **kommt**	= he, she or it *comes*
	(gate) **geht**	= he, she or it *goes*
	(lairnt) **lernt**	= he, she or it *learns*
	(browkt) **braucht**	= he, she or it *needs*
	(haht) **hat***	= he, she or it *has*
	(murk-tah) **möchte***	= he, she or it *would like*

Note:
- With **ich** you drop the final "n" from the basic verb form.
- With **er, sie,** or **es** you drop the final "en" of the basic verb form and substitute "t" instead.

*Some **Verben** just will not conform to the rules! But don't worry . . . you will be perfectly understood whether you say **„hat"** or **„habt."** Germans will be delighted that you have taken the time to learn the language.

- ☐ **der Mund** *(moont)* . . . . mouth ______________
- ☐ **das Museum** *(moo-zay-oom)* . . . . museum ______________
- ☐ **die Musik** *(moo-zeek)* . . . . music ______________
- ☐ **die Mutter** *(moo-tair)* . . . . mother ______________
- ☐ **nächst** *(nexst)* . . . . next ______________

With ,,**wir**,“ *(vir)* we ,,**Sie**,“ *(zee)* you or ,,**sie**,“ *(zee)* they there is no change at all!

wir / **Sie** / **sie**	**kommen**	= we, you, or they *come*	**brauchen**	=	we, you, or they *need*
	gehen	= we, you, or they *go*	**haben**	=	we, you, or they *have*
	lernen	= we, you, or they *learn*	**möchten**	=	we, you, or they *would like*

Note: **Sie** only **haben zwei** changes to remember.

ich is followed by verbs with an “e” on the end . . . . *ex.* **ich brauche**

er, sie, es are followed by verbs with a “t” on the end . . . . *ex.* **er braucht**
sie braucht
es braucht

Deutsche verbs are easy. At the back of **das** *(boohk)* **Buch,** *(zee)* **Sie** will find *(zee-ben)* **sieben** *(zigh-ten)* **Seiten** of flash cards to help **Sie** learn these *(noy-ah)* **neue** *(vur-tair)* **Wörter.** Cut them out, carry them in your briefcase, purse, pocket *(oh-dair)* **oder** knapsack; *(oont)* **und** review them whenever **Sie** *(hah-ben)* **haben** a free moment.

Nun fill in the following blanks **mit** the correct form of the verb shown. Each time **Sie** write out the sentence, be sure *(owk)* **auch** to say it aloud.

(lair-nen)
lernen
to learn

Ich ______________________ *(doych)* **Deutsch.**

Er / Sie / Es lernt **Deutsch.**

Wir ______________________ **Deutsch.**

Sie (you) ______________________ *(eng-leash)* **Englisch.**

Sie (they) ______________________ **Deutsch.**

(koh-men)
kommen
to come

Ich ______________________ **aus** *(ah-mair-ih-kah)* **Amerika.**

Er / Sie / Es ______________________ **aus Amerika.**

Wir ______________________ **aus** *(hole-lahnt)* **Holland.**

Sie (you) kommen **aus** *(eng-lahnt)* **England.**

Sie (they) ______________ **aus Deutschland.**

☐ **die Nacht** *(nahkt)* . . . . night ______________
— ex. **,,Gute Nacht!“** ______________
☐ **der Name** *(nah-mah)* . . . . name ______________
☐ **die Nation** *(nah-tsi-ohn)* . . . . nation ______________
☐ **die Nationalität** *(nah-tsi-oh-nahl-ih-tate)* nationality ______________

(gay-en)
gehen
to go

Ich ______________ **nach Deutschland.**
Er
Sie ______________ **nach Italien.**
Es
Wir ______________ **nach Holland.**

Sie (you) ______________ **nach England.**

Sie (they) gehen ______________ **nach China.**

(brow-ken)
brauchen
to need

Ich ______________ **ein** *(tsi-mair)* **Zimmer.**
Er
Sie ______________ **ein Zimmer.**
Es
Wir brauchen ______________ **ein Zimmer.**

Sie (you) ______________ **ein Zimmer.**

Sie (they) ______________ **ein Zimmer.**

(hah-ben)
haben
to have

Ich habe ______________ **fünf Mark.**
Er
Sie ______________ **sechs Mark.**
Es
Wir ______________ **zehn Mark.**

Sie (you) ______________ **zwei Mark.**

Sie (they) ______________ **drei Mark.**

(murk-ten)
möchten
would like

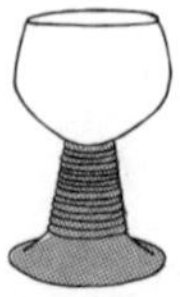

Ich ______________ **ein Glas Wein.**
Er
Sie ______________ **eine** *(tah-sah)* **Tasse** (cup) *(kah-kow)* **Kakao.** (hot chocolate)
Es
Wir ______________ **ein Glas Weißwein.**

Sie (you) ______________ **ein Glas Milch.**

Sie (they) möchten ______________ **ein Glas Bier.**

Hier sind *(zex)* **sechs** more **Verben.**

(high-sen) **heißen** = to be called

____

(kow-fen) **kaufen** = to buy

____

(shprek-en) **sprechen** = to speak

____

(voh-nen) **wohnen** = to live/reside

____

(be-stel-en) **bestellen** = to order

____

(bly-ben) **bleiben** = to stay/remain

bleiben ______________

- ☐ **natürlich** *(nah-tewr-leehk)* .... naturally ______________
- ☐ **der November** *(noh-vem-bair)* .... November ______________
- ☐ **die Nummer** *(noo-mair)* .... number ______________
- ☐ **der Ofen** *(oh-fen)* .... oven ______________
- ☐ **oft** *(ohft)* .... often ______________

Nun, fill in the following blanks **mit** the correct form of each verb. Be sure to say each sentence out loud until **Sie haben es** down pat!

(high-sen)
heißen
to be called

Ich __________ **Doktor Müller.**
Er / Sie / Es __________ **Zimmermann.**
Wir __________ **Faber.**
Sie (you) __________ **Holtzheimer.**
Sie (they) heißen **Familie Nickel.**

(kow-fen)
kaufen
to buy

Ich kaufe **ein Buch.**
Er / Sie / Es __________ **einen Salat.**
Wir __________ **ein Auto.**
Sie (you) __________ **eine Uhr.**
Sie (they) __________ **eine Lampe.**

(shprek-en)
sprechen
to be called

Ich __________ **Deutsch.**
Er / Sie / Es __________ **Englisch.**
Wir __________ **Spanisch.**
Sie (you) sprechen **Dänisch.**
Sie (they) __________ **Japanisch.**

(voh-nen)
wohnen
to live/reside

Ich wohne **in Deutschland.**
Er / Sie / Es __________ **in Amerika.**
Wir __________ **in einem Hotel.**
Sie (you) __________ **in Europa.**
Sie (they) __________ **in Japan.**

(be-stel-en)
bestellen
to order

Ich __________ **ein Glas Wasser.**
Er / Sie / Es __________ **ein Glas Wein.**
Wir bestellen **eine Tasse Tee.**
Sie (you) __________ **eine Tasse Kaffee.**
Sie (they) __________ **ein Glas Milch.**

(bly-ben)
bleiben
to stay/remain

Ich __________ **noch** *(nohk)* still **fünf Tage.**
Er / Sie / Es bleibt **noch drei Tage.**
Wir __________ **noch sechs Tage.**
Sie (you) __________ **noch sieben Tage.**
Sie (they) __________ **noch acht Tage.**

☐ **offen** *(ohf-fen)* . . . . open __________
— ex. **Das Restaurant ist offen.** __________
☐ **der Offizier** *(oh-fih-tseer)* . . . . officer __________
— ex. **Der Offizier ist um die Ecke.** __________
☐ **der Oktober** *(ohk-toh-bair)* . . . . October __________

Nun see if *(zee)* **Sie** can fill in the blanks below. The correct answers *(zint)* **sind** at the bottom of the *(zigh-tah)* **Seite.**

1. I speak German. ____________________
2. He comes from America. ____________________
3. We learn German. ____________________
4. They have 10 marks. ____________________
5. She would like a glass of water. ____________________
6. We need a room. ____________________
7. I am called Faber. ____________________
8. I live in America. ____________________
9. You are buying a book. Sie kaufen ein Buch.
10. He orders a beer. ____________________

In the following Steps, *(zee)* **Sie** will be introduced to more **und** more **Verben und** should drill them in exactly the same way as **Sie** did in this section. Look up **neue Wörter** in your *(vur-tair-boohk)* **Wörterbuch** (dictionary) **und** make up your own sentences using the same type of pattern. Remember, the more **Sie** practice **nun**, the more enjoyable your trip will be. **Viel Glück!**

Nun ist a perfect time to turn to the back of **das Buch,** clip out your flash cards, and start flashing.

Be sure to check off your free **Wörter** in the box provided as **Sie lernen** each one.

ANTWORTEN

1. **Ich spreche Deutsch.**
2. **Er kommt aus Amerika.**
3. **Wir lernen Deutsch.**
4. **Sie haben zehn Mark.**
5. **Sie möchte ein Glas Wasser.**
6. **Wir brauchen ein Zimmer.**
7. **Ich heiße Faber.**
8. **Ich wohne in Amerika.**
9. **Sie kaufen ein Buch.**
10. **Er bestellt ein Bier.**

Step 12

(mih-noo-ten) die Minuten
minutes

Sie know *(vee)* **wie** to tell **die** *(tah-gah)* **Tage** of the *(voh-kah)* **Woche und die** *(moh-nah-tah)* **Monate** of the **Jahr,** so **nun** let's learn to tell time. Punctuality **in Deutschland ist sehr** *(veehk-teeg)* **wichtig,** not to mention the need of catching *(tsew-gah)* **Züge** (trains) **und** arriving on time. **Hier sind** the "basics."

What time is it? = *(vee) (shpayt)* **Wie spät ist es?** / *(vee-feel) (uhr)* **Wieviel Uhr ist es?**

before = *(for)* **vor** vor

after = *(nahk)* **nach** ______________

half = *(hahlp)* **halb** ______________

Es ist *(fewnf)* **fünf Uhr.**

Es ist *(hahlp)* **halb fünf.**

Es ist *(dry)* **drei Uhr.**

Es ist halb drei.

Es ist *(tsvahn-tsig)* **zwanzig Minuten** *(nahk)* **nach** *(ahkt)* **acht.** **ODER** **Es ist acht Uhr zwanzig.**

Es ist zwanzig Minuten *(for)* **vor acht.** **ODER** **Es ist** *(zee-ben)* **sieben Uhr** *(fear-tsig)* **vierzig.**

Nun fill in the blanks according to the *(tsight)* **Zeit** (time) indicated on the *(uhr)* **Uhr** (clock). The answers **sind** below.

Es ist ______________.

Es ist ______________.

Es ist ______________.

Es ist ______________.

Es ist ______________.

Es ist vier Uhr.

Es ist ______________.

Es ist ______________.

ANTWORTEN

Es ist zehn Uhr zehn.
Es ist zwanzig Minuten nach zwei.
Es ist halb acht.
Es ist sechs Uhr zehn.
(Es ist zehn Minuten nach sechs.)

Es ist halb zwei.
Es ist vier Uhr.
Es ist zwanzig Minuten nach zwölf.
Es ist zehn Minuten vor sechs.
(Es ist fünf Uhr fünfzig.)

Hier sind more time-telling **Wörter** to add to your **Wort** power.

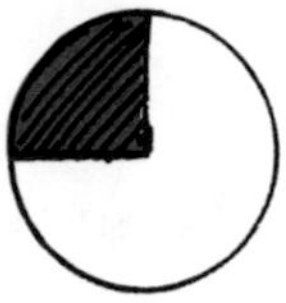

ein Viertel *(fear-tel)*	=	a quarter
ein Viertel vor	=	a quarter before
ein Viertel nach	=	a quarter after

Es ist ein Viertel *(fear-tel)* **nach zwei** *(tsvai)*. **ODER** **Es ist zwei Uhr fünfzehn** *(fewnf-tsayn)*.

Es ist ein Viertel vor zwei. **ODER** **Es ist ein Uhr fünfundvierzig** *(fewnf-oont-fear-tsig)*.

Nun es ist your turn.

Es ist ______________________.

Es ist ______________________.

Es ist ein Viertel vor drei.

Es ist ______________________.

See how **wichtig** *(veehk-teeg)* (important) learning **die Nummern ist? Nun** answer the following **Fragen** *(frah-gen)* (questions) based on the **Uhren** below. The answers **sind** at the bottom of the **Seite**.

Wie spät ist es? *(vee) (shpayt)*

1 

2 

3 

4 

5 

6 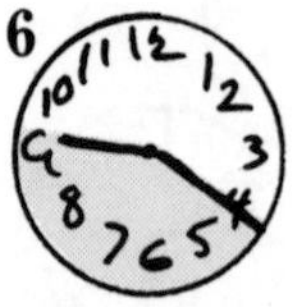

7 

1. Es ist sechs Uhr.
2. ______________________
3. ______________________
4. ______________________
5. ______________________
6. ______________________
7. ______________________

ANTWORTEN

1. **Es ist sechs Uhr.**
2. **Es ist halb acht.**
   Es ist sieben Uhr dreißig.
3. **Es ist acht Uhr.**
4. **Es ist halb zwei.**
   Es ist ein Uhr dreißig.
5. **Es ist ein Viertel nach zwölf.**
   Es ist zwölf Uhr fünfzehn.
6. **Es ist zwanzig Minuten nach neun.**
   Es ist vierzig Minuten vor zehn.
7. **Es ist siebzehn Minuten nach zwei.**
   Es ist dreiundvierzig Minuten vor drei.

When **Sie** *(zee)* answer a „**Wann**“ *(vahn)* question, say „**um**“ *(oom)* (at) before you give the time.

Wann *(vahn)* **kommt der Zug** *(tsook)*? um sechs Uhr.

Nun answer the following **Fragen** *(frah-gen)* based on the **Uhren** below. Be sure to practice saying each question out loud several times.

Wann *(vahn)* **beginnt** *(bay-gint)* **das Konzert** *(kohn-tsairt)*? ____________________.

Wann beginnt das Theater *(tay-ah-tair)*? ____________________.

Wann kommt der *(dair)* **gelbe Bus** *(boos)*? ____________________.

Wann kommt das Taxi *(tahx-ee)*? um halb fünf.

Wann *(vahn)* **ist das Restaurant auf** *(owf)* (open)? ____________________.

Wann ist das Restaurant zu *(tsoo)* (closed)? ____________________.

Um *(oom)* (at) **acht Uhr morgens sagt** *(zahkt)* (says) **man** *(mahn)* (one),
„Guten Morgen, Frau (Mrs.) **Bernhard!“**

Um *(oom)* (at) **acht Uhr abends sagt man,**
„Guten Abend, Fräulein *(froy-line)* (Miss) **Seehafer!”**

Um *(oom)* **ein Uhr nachmittags** *(nahk-mit-tahgs)* **sagt man,**
„Guten Tag, Herr *(hair)* (Mr.) **Richter** *(reek-tair)*!“

Um *(oom)* **zehn Uhr abends sagt man,**
„Gute *(goo-tah)* **Nacht!“**

- ☐ **das Ohr** *(or)* .... ear ____________________
- ☐ **der Ohrring** *(or-ring)* .... earring ____________________
- ☐ **das Öl** *(url)* .... oil ____________________
- ☐ **das Omelett** *(oh-mih-let)* .... omelette ____________________
- ☐ **der Onkel** *(ohn-kel)* .... uncle ____________________

Remember:

What time is it? =	**Wie spät ist es?** / **Wieviel Uhr ist es?**
When/at what time =	**Wann** / **Um wieviel Uhr**

Can **Sie** pronounce **und** understand the following paragraph?

> **Der Zug von Stuttgart kommt um 15:15. Es ist nun 15:20. Der Zug** *(tsook)* **ist spät. Der Zug** *(tsook)* **kommt heute um 17:15. Morgen kommt der Zug wieder** *(vee-dair)* (again) **um 15:15.**

Hier sind more practice exercises. Answer **die Fragen** *(frah-gen)* (questions) based on the **Zeit** *(tsight)* given.

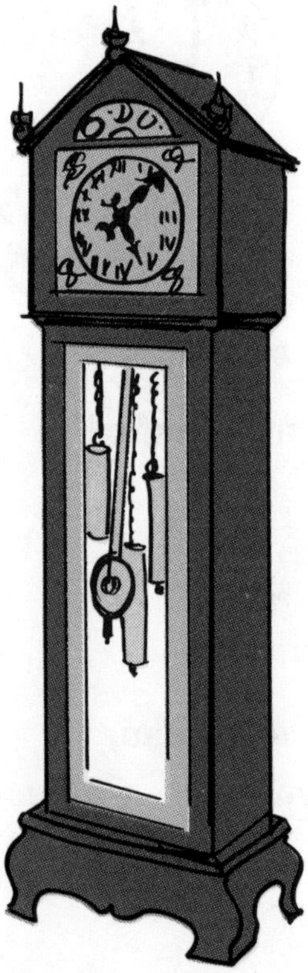

Wieviel Uhr ist es?

1. (10:30) ______________________
2. (6:30) ______________________
3. (2:15) ______________________
4. (11:40) Es ist elf Uhr vierzig.
5. (12:18) ______________________
6. (7:20) ______________________
7. (3:10) ______________________
8. (4:05) ______________________
9. (5:35) ______________________
10. (11:50) ______________________

- ☐ **die Oper** *(oh-pair)*. . . . . opera ____________
  - — ex. **Ich gehe in die Oper.** ____________
- ☐ **das Opernhaus** *(oh-pairn-house)*. . . . . . . opera house ____________
  - — ex. **Das Opernhaus ist sehr groß.** ____________
- ☐ **die Ordnung** *(ohrd-noong)*. . . . . order ____________

(here) **Hier ist** a quick quiz. Fill in the blanks **mit den** *(reehk-tee-gen)* **richtigen** (correct) **Nummern.** The answers **sind unten.**

1. **Eine Minute hat** ______ (?) *(zay-koon-den)* **Sekunden.** (seconds)
2. **Eine Stunde** (hour) **hat** ______ (?) **Minuten.**
3. **Ein Tag hat** ______ (?) *(shtoon-den)* **Stunden.** (hours)
4. **Eine Woche hat** sieben (?) **Tage.**
5. **Ein** *(moh-naht)* **Monat hat** ______ (?) *(tah-gah)* **Tage.**
6. **Ein Jahr hat** ______ (?) **Monate.**
7. **Ein Jahr hat** ______ (?) *(voh-ken)* **Wochen.**
8. **Ein Jahr hat** ______ (?) **Tage.**

Hier ist a sample **Seite von** *(ine-em)* **einem deutschen Zugfahrplan** (train schedule)**.** **Ein** *(tay-ay-ay)* **TEE-Zug ist sehr schnell** (fast)**.** **Ein** *(day)* **D-Zug ist schnell, und ein** *(ay)* **E-Zug ist** *(long-zahm)* **langsam** (slow)**.** Which **Zug** would **Sie** prefer to take?

von Heidelberg nach Frankfurt

(ahp) **ab** leaves	**Zug #**	*(on)* **an** arrives	*(bih-mair-koong-en)* **Bemerkungen** notes
7:40	TEE 40	8:30	
10:00	D 16	11:10	
12:15	D 38	13:25	
14:32	E 693	16:15	

ANTWORTEN

1. sechzig 2. sechzig 3. vierundzwanzig 4. sieben 5. dreißig 6. zwölf 7. zweiundfünfzig 8. dreihundert-fünfundsechzig

Hier sind die *(noy-en)* **neuen Verben für** Step 12.

(zah-gen) **sagen** = to say | *(es-sen)* **essen** = to eat | *(trink-en)* **trinken** = to drink

_______________ essen _______________ _______________

(zah-gen) **sagen** (to say)

Ich _______________ **das** *(hoy-tah)* **heute.**

Er
Sie _______________ *(feel)* **viel** (much) **heute.**
Es

Wir sagen _______________ *(nine)* **„nein."** (no)

Sie _______________ **„ja."** (yes)

Sie _______________ *(neehk-ts)* **nichts.** (nothing)

(es-sen) **essen** (to eat)

Ich _______________ *(vee-nair)* **Wiener** *(shnit-tsel)* **Schnitzel.**

Er
Sie _______________ *(fish)* **Fisch.**
Es

Wir _______________ **eine** *(zoo-pah)* **Suppe.** (soup)

Sie (you) essen _______________ **ein Beefsteak.**

Sie (they) _______________ *(lahm)* **Lamm.** (lamb)

(trink-en) **trinken** (to drink)

Ich _______________ *(milsh)* **Milch.**

Er
Sie trinkt _______________ *(vice-vine)* **Weißwein.**
Es

Wir _______________ **Mineralwasser.**

Sie _______________ *(toh-mah-ten-zahft)* **Tomatensaft.** (tomato juice)

Sie _______________ *(kah-kow)* **Kakao.** (hot chocolate)

Remember that **„ei"** is pronounced like "eye" or like the "i" in "mine."

☐ **das Orchester** *(or-kes-tair)*................ orchestra _______________
— ex. **Das Orchester in New York ist sehr groß.** _______________
☐ **die Organization** *(ohr-gahn-ih-zah-tsi-ohn)* .. organization _______________
☐ **die Orgel** *(or-gell)*...................... organ _______________
— ex. **Die Orgel ist sehr alt.** _______________

(bilt)
das Bild

(deck-ah)
die Decke

(eck-ah)
die Ecke

(fen-stair)
das Fenster

(lahm-pah)
die Lampe

(leeht)
das Licht

(zoh-fah)
das Sofa

(shtool)
der Stuhl

(tep-eeh)
der Teppich

(tish)
der Tisch

(tewr)
die Tür

(uhr)
die Uhr

(for-hahng)
der Vorhang

(vahnt)
die Wand

(house)
das Haus

(es-tsi-mair)
das Eßzimmer

(vohn-tsi-mair)
das Wohnzimmer

(shlahf-tsi-mair)
das Schlafzimmer

(bah-da-tsi-mair)
das Badezimmer

(kew-sha)
die Küche

(bew-roh)
das Büro

(kel-lair)
der Keller

(ga-rah-zha)
die Garage

(ow-toe)
das Auto

(vah-gen)
der Wagen

(fahr-raht)
das Fahrrad

(hoont)
der Hund

(kaht-tsa)
die Katze

(gar-ten)
der Garten

(bloo-men)
die Blumen

(breef-kah-sten)
der Briefkasten

(post)
die Post

(kling-el)
die Klingel

(ines)
1 eins

(tsvai)
2 zwei

(dry)
3 drei

(fear)
4 vier

(fewnf)
5 fünf

(zex)
6 sechs

(zee-ben)
7 sieben

(ahkt)
8 acht

(noyn)
9 neun

(tsayn)
10 zehn

(vice)
weiß

(shvarts)
schwarz

(gelp)
gelb

(roht)
rot

(blau)
blau

(grau)
grau

(brown)
braun

(grewn)
grün

(roh-zah)
rosa

(boont)
bunt

(zohn-tahk)
der Sonntag

(mohn-tahk)
der Montag

(deens-tahk)
der Dienstag

(mit-vohk)
der Mittwoch

(doh-nairs-tahk)
der Donnerstag

(fry-tahk)
der Freitag

(zahms-tahk)
der Samstag

(goo-ten) (more-gen)
Guten Morgen

(goo-ten) (tahk)
Guten Tag

(goo-ten) (ah-bent)
Guten Abend

(goo-tah) (nahkt)
Gute Nacht

(kewl-shrahnk)
der Kühlschrank

(oh-fen)
der Ofen

(vine)
der Wein

(beer)
das Bier

(milsh)
die Milch

(boo-tair)
die Butter

(tell-air)
der Teller

(mes-sair)
das Messer

(gah-bel)
die Gabel

(lur-fel)
der Löffel

(zair-vee-et-tah)
die Serviette

(tah-sah)
die Tasse

(glahs)
das Glas

(zahlts)
das Salz

(fef-air)
der Pfeffer

(shrahnk)
der Schrank

STICKY LABELS

This book has over 150 special sticky labels for you to use as you learn new words. When you are introduced to a word, remove the corresponding label from these pages. Be sure to use each of these unique labels by adhering them to a picture, window, lamp, or whatever object it refers to. The sticky labels make learning to speak German much more fun and a lot easier than you ever expected.

For example, when you look in the mirror and see the label, say

(dair) *(shpee-gel)*
"der Spiegel."

Don't just say it once, say it again and again.

And once you label the refrigerator, you should never again open that door without saying

(dair) *(kewl-shrahnk)*
"der Kühlschrank."

By using the sticky labels, you not only learn new words but friends and family learn along with you!

(broht)
das **Brot**

(tay)
der **Tee**

(kah-fay)
der **Kaffee**

(vah-sair)
das **Wasser**

(kah-kow)
der **Kakao**

(bet)
das **Bett**

(bet-deck-ah)
die **Bettdecke**

(kohpf-kiss-en)
das **Kopfkissen**

(veck-air)
der **Wecker**

(kly-dair-shrahnk)
der **Kleiderschrank**

(vahsh-beck-en)
das **Waschbecken**

(doosh-ah)
die **Dusche**

(toy-let-tah)
die **Toilette**

(toohk)
das **Tuch**

(hahnt-toohk)
das **Handtuch**

(bah-dah-toohk)
das **Badetuch**

(vahsh-lah-pen)
der **Waschlappen**

(shpee-gel)
der **Spiegel**

(bly-shtift)
der **Bleistift**

(koo-lee)
der **Kuli**

(pah-peer)
das **Papier**

(pah-peer-kohrp)
der **Papierkorb**

(breef)
der **Brief**

(breef-mahr-kah)
die **Briefmarke**

(boohk)
das **Buch**

(post-kar-tah)
die **Postkarte**

(tsight-shrift)
die **Zeitschrift**

(tsigh-toong)
die **Zeitung**

(bril-ah)
die **Brille**

(fairn-zay-air)
der **Fernseher**

(pah-ss)
der **Paß**

(flook-kar-tah)
die **Flugkarte**

(gelt)
das **Geld**

(kah-mair-ah)
die **Kamera**

(film)
der **Film**

(koh-fair)
der **Koffer**

(breef-tah-shah)
die **Brieftasche**

(hahnt-tah-shah)
die **Handtasche**

(bah-da-on-tsook)
der **Badeanzug**

(zahn-dah-len)
die **Sandalen**

(zigh-fah)
die **Seife**

(tsahn-bewr-stah)
die **Zahnbürste**

(tsahn-pah-stah)
die **Zahnpaste**

(kahm)
der **Kamm**

(mahn-tel)
der **Mantel**

(ray-gen-mahn-tel)
der **Regenmantel**

(ray-gen-shirm)
der **Regenschirm**

(hahnt-shoo-ah)
die **Handschuhe**

(hoot)
der **Hut**

(shoo-ah)
die **Schuhe**

(shtee-fel)
die **Stiefel**

(zoh-ken)
die **Socken**

(shtroompf-hoh-zah)
die **Strumpfhose**

(shlahf-on-tsook)
der **Schlafanzug**

(nahkt-hemt)
das **Nachthemd**

(house-shoo-ah)
die **Hausschuhe**

(bah-da-mahn-tel)
der **Bademantel**

(on-tsook)
der **Anzug**

(krah-vah-tah)
die **Krawatte**

(tah-shen-toohk)
das **Taschentuch**

(yah-kah)
die **Jacke**

(hoh-zah)
die **Hose**

(hemt)
das **Hemd**

(klite)
das **Kleid**

(rohk)
der **Rock**

(bloo-zah)
die **Bluse**

(pool-ee)
der **Pulli**

(oon-tair-hoh-zah)
die **Unterhose**

(oon-tair-hemt)
das **Unterhemd**

(oon-tair-rohk)
der **Unterrock**

(bay-hah)
der **BH**

(goo-ten) (ah-pe-teet)
Guten Appetit!

(be-zetst)
besetzt

(ent-shool-dee-goong)
Entschuldigung

(eehk) (bin) (ah-mair-ih-kahn-air)
Ich bin Amerikaner.

(eehk) (murk-tah) (doych) (lair-nen)
Ich möchte Deutsch lernen.

(eehk) (high-sah)
Ich heiße __________.

PLUS . . .

Your book includes a number of other innovative features. At the back of the book, you'll find seven pages of flash cards. Cut them out and flip through them at least once a day.

On pages 112 and 113, you'll find a beverage guide and a menu guide. Don't wait until your trip to use them. Clip out the menu guide and use it tonight at the dinner table. And use the beverage guide to practice ordering your favorite drinks.

By using the special features in this book, you will be speaking German before you know it.

(feel) (shpahss)
Viel Spaß!
have fun

(nort) Nord - *(zewt)* Süd, *(ohst)* Ost - *(vest)* West
north - south, east - west

Step 13

If **Sie** are looking at a **Landkarte** *(lahnt-kar-tah)* (map) **und Sie** see the following **Wörter, es** should **nicht** *(neehkt)* (not) be too difficult to figure out **was sie** *(zee)* (they) mean. Take an educated guess. The answers **sind** below.

(nort-zay) **die Nordsee**	*(ohst-zay)* **die Ostsee**	*(ohst-bear-leen)* **Ostberlin**
(nort-leehkt) **das Nordlicht**	*(nort-kahp)* **das Nordkap**	*(vest-bear-leen)* **Westberlin**
(nort-ah-mair-ih-kah) **das Nordamerika**	*(zewt-ah-mair-ih-kah)* **das Südamerika**	*(zewt-pole)* **der Südpol**
(nort-pole) **der Nordpol**	*(ohst-ah-zee-en)* **das Ostasien**	*(zewt-ah-free-kah)* **das Südafrika**

Die deutschen Wörter für north, south, east **und** west **sind** easy to recognize due to their similarity to **Englisch.** So . . .

(nor-den) **der Norden**	=	the north	________
(zew-den) **der Süden**	=	the south	der Süden
(oh-sten) **der Osten**	=	the east	________
(ves-ten) **der Westen**	=	the west	________

(nurt-leehk) **nördlich**	=	northern	________
(zewt-leehk) **südlich**	=	southern	________
(ohst-leehk) **ostlich**	=	eastern	________
(vest-leehk) **westlich**	=	western	westlich

Der Westen ist often the phrase used to refer to the American Wild West. **Der Osten** by comparison **ist** frequently used by West Germans when referring to East Germany.

But what about more basic directions such as "left," "right," "straight ahead" **und** "around the corner"? Let's learn these **Wörter nun.**

links
left

(rex)
rechts
right

straight ahead	=	*(ge-rah-dah-ows)* **geradeaus**
around the corner	=	*(oom)* **um die** *(eck-ah)* **Ecke**
on the right side	=	*(owf)* **auf der** *(reck-ten)* **rechten Seite**
on the left side	=	**auf der linken Seite**

ANTWORTEN

the North Sea	**the East Sea** = **Baltic Sea**	**East Berlin**
the Northern Lights	**the North Cap**	**West Berlin**
North America	**South America**	**the South Pole**
the North Pole	**East Asia**	**South Africa**

Just as **auf Englisch**, these **drei Wörter** go a long way.

(bit-tah) **bitte**	= please
(dahn-kah) **danke**	= thank you danke
(ent-shool-dee-goong) **Entschuldigung**	= excuse me

(tsvai) *(two-pish-ah)* *(kohn-fair-zah-tsi-oh-nen)*
Hier sind zwei sehr typische Konversationen für someone who is trying to find something.
typical

Karl: *(ent-shool-dee-goong)* **Entschuldigung. Wo ist das Hotel Ritter?** *(rih-tair)* knight

Heinz: **Gehen** *(gay-en)* go **Sie zwei Straßen weiter** *(vhy-tair)* further**, dann links, dann geradeaus. Sie finden dann das Hotel Ritter.**

Karl: **Entschuldigung. Wo ist das Deutsche Museum?**

Helga: **Gehen Sie geradeaus und dann rechts um die Ecke. Ungefähr** *(oon-ge-fair)* approximately **hundert Meter weiter** *(vhy-tair)* **auf der linken Seite ist das Deutsche Museum.**

Are you lost? There is no need to be lost if **Sie haben** learned the basic direction **Wörter**. Do not try to memorize these **Konversationen** because you will never be looking for precisely these places! One day you might need to ask for directions to **„das Restaurant zur Sonne"** **oder „das Goethe Museum" oder „das Hotel Europa."** Learn the key direction **Wörter** and be sure **Sie** can find your destination.

What if the person responding to your **Frage** answers too quickly for you to understand the entire reply? If so, ask again, saying,

- ☐ **der Ozean** *(oh-tsay-on)* .... ocean
  — ex. **Der Ozean ist blau und grün.**
- ☐ **ein paar** *(par)* .... a pair/a couple
- ☐ **packen** *(pah-ken)* .... to pack
- ☐ **das Paket** *(pah-kate)* .... package

(ent-shool-dee-goong) **Entschuldigung.** **Ich bin Amerikaner und ich spreche** *(noor)* **nur** (only) **ein** (a) *(bis-hen)* **bißchen** (little) **Deutsch.**

Sprechen (speak) **Sie bitte** *(long-zah-mair)* **langsamer** (slower). *(vee-dair-hoh-len)* **Wiederholen** (repeat) **Sie das** (that) **bitte.**

Nun when the directions are repeated, **Sie** will be able to understand if **Sie haben** learned the key **Wörter** for directions. Quiz yourself by filling in the blanks below **mit** *(dane)* **den richtigen deutschen Wörtern**.

Liesel: **Entschuldigung. Wo ist das Restaurant** *(zay-blick)* **Seeblick** (sea view)**?**

Johannes: *(gay-en)* **Gehen Sie** ________ (three) ________ (streets) ________ (further), *(don)* **dann** ________ (left)

um (around) ________ (the) ________ (corner), **dann** ________ (straight ahead).

Dort ist eine Kirche. Dann ________ (right) ________ (around) ________ (the)

________ (corner). Auf (On) ________ (the) ________ (left) ________ (side)

ist das Restaurant *(zay-blick)* **Seeblick** (sea view). **Viel Glück.**

Hier sind vier neue Verben.

(shtay-en) **stehen** = to stand ________

(fair-shtay-en) **verstehen** = to understand ________

(fair-kow-fen) **verkaufen** = to sell verkaufen

(vee-dair-hoh-len) **wiederholen** = to repeat ________

- ☐ **das Papier** *(pah-peer)*................ paper ________
- ☐ **der Park** *(park)*.................... park ________
- ☐ **der Passagier** *(pah-sa-zheer)*.......... passenger ________
- ☐ **der Paß** *(pah-ss)*.................... passport ________
- ☐ **die Paßkontrolle** *(pah-ss-kohn-troll-ah)* passport control ________

As always, say each sentence out loud. Say each and every **Wort** carefully, pronouncing everything **Sie** see.

(shtay-en)
stehen
to stand

Ich stehe **auf der linken Seite.**
Er / Sie / Es ________ **hinter dem Haus.**
Wir ________ **vor dem Haus.**
Sie (you) ________ **neben dem Haus.**
Sie (they) ________ **auf dem Haus.**

(fair-shtay-en)
verstehen
to understand

Ich ________ **Deutsch.**
Er / Sie / Es ________ **Englisch.**
Wir ________ **Dänisch.**
Sie verstehen **Italienisch.**
Sie ________ *(roo-sish)* **Russisch.**

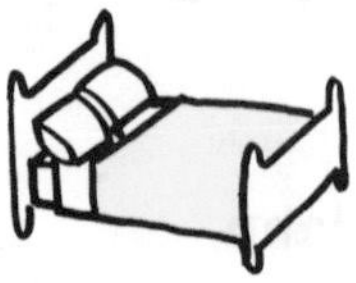

(fair-kow-fen)
verkaufen
to sell

Ich ________ **das Bett.**
Er / Sie / Es ________ **die grüne Jacke.**
Wir ________ **den neuen Film.**
Sie ________ **den guten Fisch.**
Sie verkaufen **viele Karten.**

(vee-dair-hoh-len)
wiederholen
to repeat

Ich wiederhole **das Wort.**
Er / Sie / Es ________ **das nicht.**
Wir ________ **das Wort nicht.**
Sie ________ **das.**
Sie ________ **das nicht.**

Nun, see if **Sie** can translate the following thoughts into **Deutsch.** The answers **sind unten.**

1. She repeats the word. ________
2. They sell tickets. Sie verkaufen Karten.
3. He stands in front of the house. ________
4. We eat fish. ________
5. I speak German. ________
6. I drink tea. ________

ANTWORTEN

1. **Sie wiederholt das Wort.**
2. **Sie verkaufen Karten.**
3. **Er steht vor dem Haus.**
4. **Wir essen Fisch.**
5. **Ich spreche Deutsch.**
6. **Ich trinke Tee.**

Oben *(oh-ben)* - Unten *(oon-ten)*
above - below

Before **Sie beginnen** Step 14, review Step 8. **Nun** *(noon)* **lernen** *(lair-nen)* **wir** *(vir)* **mehr.**

Hier ist ein Haus in Deutschland *(doych-lahnt)*.

Das Schlafzimmer *(shlahf-tsi-mair)* (bedroom) **ist oben** *(oh-ben)*.

Das Badezimmer *(bah-da-tsi-mair)* (bathroom) **ist auch oben.**

Das Büro *(bew-roh)* **ist unten** *(oon-ten)*.

Das Wohnzimmer *(vohn-tsi-mair)* (living room) **ist auch unten.**

Gehen *(gay-en)* (go) **Sie nun in** your **Schlafzimmer** *(shlahf-tsi-mair)* **und** look around **das Zimmer** *(tsi-mair)*. Let's learn **die Namen** of the **Dinge in dem Schlafzimmer** just like **wir** *(vir)* learned the various parts of the **Haus.** Be sure to practice saying **die Wörter** as you **schreiben** *(shry-ben)* (write) them in the spaces **unten.** Also say out loud the example sentences **unter** *(oon-tair)* **den Bildern.**

das Bett *(bet)*

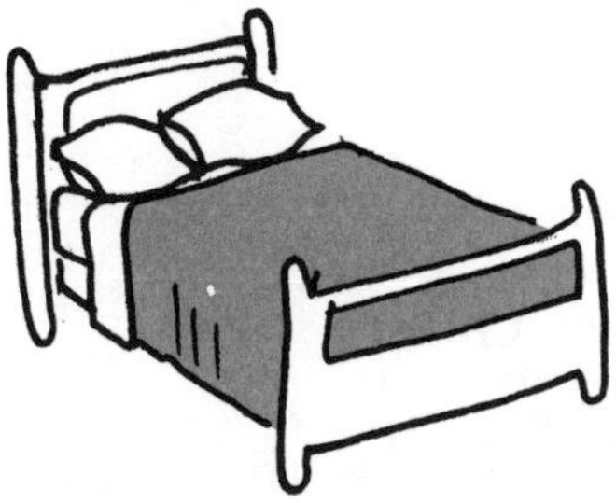

____

Ich kaufe das Bett.

die Bettdecke *(bet-deck-ah)*
blanket

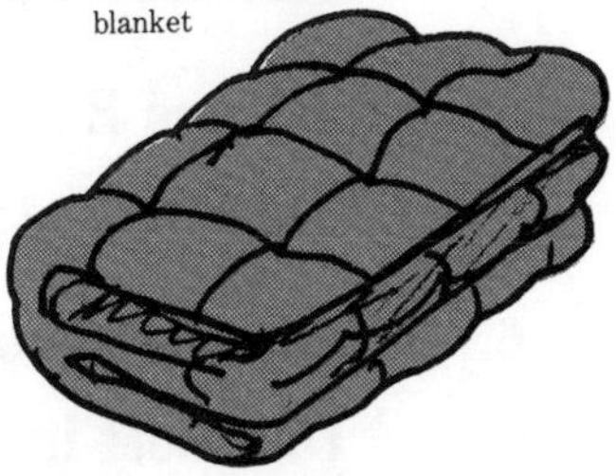

die Bettdecke

Ich brauche *(brow-kah)* (need) **eine Bettdecke.**

das Kopfkissen *(kohpf-kiss-en)*
pillow

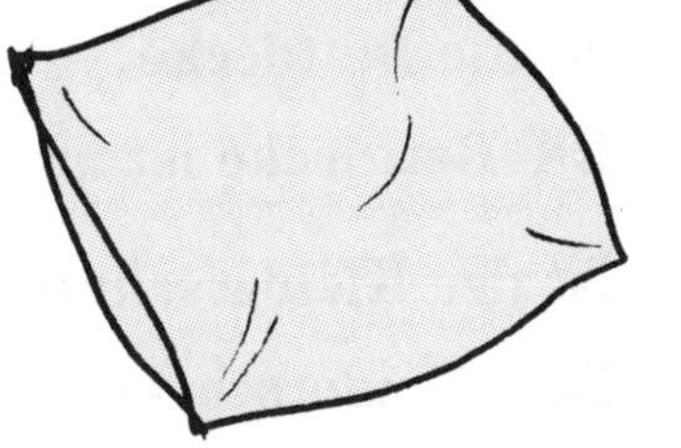

____

Das Kopfkissen ist sehr groß.

☐ **der Pfeffer** *(fef-air)*	pepper	______________
☐ **das Pfund** *(foont)*	pound	______________
☐ **das Photo** *(foh-toh)*	photograph	______________
☐ **die Physik** *(fih-zeek)*	physics	______________
☐ **die Pille** *(pil-ah)*	pill	______________

(veck-air)
der Wecker

(kly-dair-shrahnk)
der Kleiderschrank

(nex-sten)
Remove **die nächsten fünf** stickers **und** label these **Dinge in** your **Schlafzimmer.**

____

(hah-bah)
Ich habe einen Wecker.

____

(shtayt)
Der Kleiderschrank steht in dem Schlafzimmer.

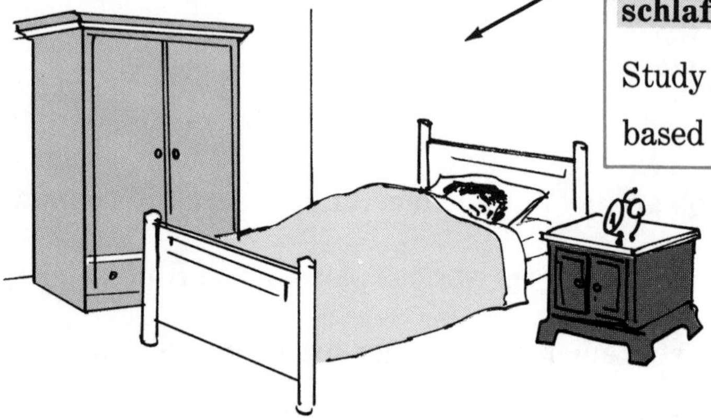

(pawn-zi-ohn)
das Schlafzimmer in einem Hotel oder Pension
(shlah-fen)
schlafen = to sleep, so a sleeping room
(frah-gen)
Study the following **Fragen und** their answers based on **das Bild links.**

1. **Wo ist der Wecker?**
   Der Wecker ist auf dem Tisch.
2. **Wo ist die Bettdecke?**
   Die Bettdecke ist auf dem Bett.
3. **Wo ist der Kleiderschrank?**
   Der Kleiderschrank steht in dem Schlafzimmer.
4. **Wo ist das Kopfkissen?**
   Das Kopfkissen ist auf dem Bett.
5. **Wo ist das Bett?**
   Das Bett steht in dem Schlafzimmer.
6. **Ist das Bett groß oder klein?** *(kline)* small
   Das Bett ist nicht groß.
   Das Bett ist klein.

- ☐ **das Polen** *(poh-len)*.................. Poland ______________
  — **wo sie sprechen Polnisch** *(pohl-nish)* ______________
- ☐ **die Police** *(poh-lee-sa)*............... policy ______________
  — like an insurance policy ______________
- ☐ **die Polizei** *(poh-li-tsigh)*............. police ______________

Nun, you answer **die Fragen** based on the previous **Bild.**

Wo ist der Wecker?

Der Wecker ist ______________________________

Wo ist das Bett?

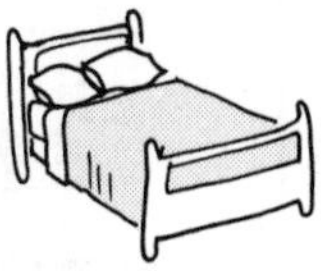

____

Let's move into **das Badezimmer und** do the same thing.

das Waschbecken *(vahsh-beck-en)*

das Waschbecken ______________________________

Das Hotelzimmer hat ein Waschbecken.

die Dusche *(doosh-ah)*

____

Die Dusche ist nicht in dem Hotelzimmer.

die Toilette *(toy-let-tah)*

____

Die Toilette ist nicht in dem Hotelzimmer. Die Toilette und die Dusche sind auf der Etage. *(eh-tah-zhah)*
on the floor

der Spiegel *(shpee-gel)* mirror ______________________________

das Tuch *(toohk)* towel das Tuch ______________________________

der Waschlappen *(vahsh-lah-pen)* washcloth ______________________________

das Handtuch *(hahnt-toohk)* hand towel ______________________________

das Badetuch *(bah-dah-toohk)* bath towel ______________________________

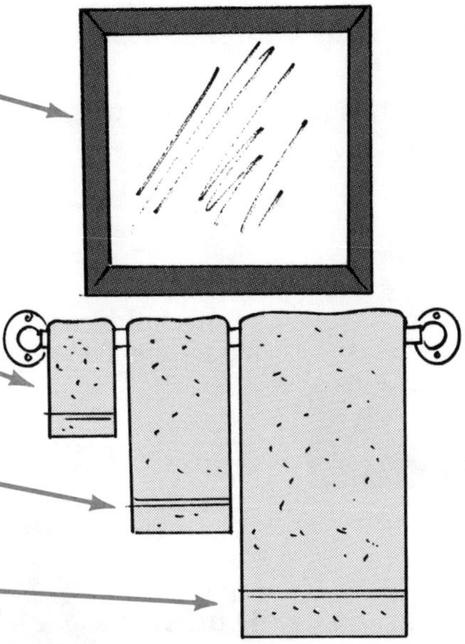

Do not forget to remove **die nächsten sieben** stickers **und** label these **Dinge** in your **Badezimmer.**

- ☐ **die Politik** *(pohl-li-teek)* .... politics ______________________________
- ☐ **das Portugal** *(pohr-too-gahl)* .... Portugal ______________________________
  — wo sie sprechen Portugiesisch *(pohr-too-gee-zish)* ______________________________
- ☐ **die Post** *(post)* .... mail ______________________________
- ☐ **die Postkarte** *(post-kar-tah)* .... postcard ______________________________

das Badezimmer in einem Haus in Europa

baden = to bathe, so a bathing room

Ist die Dusche auf der rechten oder auf der linken Seite in dem Bild? Die Dusche ist auf der ________________ (?) Seite.

Wo ist die *(toy-let-tah)* **Toilette oben? Die Toilette ist in der** *(mit-tah)* **Mitte** (middle)**.**

Wo ist das *(vahsh-beck-en)* **Waschbecken oben? Das Waschbecken ist auf der ________________ (?) Seite.**

Wo ist der *(shpee-gel)* **Spiegel oben? Der Spiegel ist über dem** Waschbecken (?)**.**

Wo sind die *(bah-dah-tewk-air)* **Badetücher** (bath towels) **in dem Bild oben?**

Die Badetücher sind über der ____________ (?). Die Badetücher sind an der ____________ (?).

Remember, **das** *(bah-da-tsi-mair)* **Badezimmer** means a room **(Zimmer)** to bathe **(baden)** in. If **Sie sind in einem Restaurant und** *(brow-ken)* **brauchen** the lavatory, **Sie** want to ask for **die Toilette** *not* for **das Badezimmer.**

Restrooms fall **unter** the title of **die Toiletten und sie** are marked **D** und **H**. **Sie** will have a sharp surprise if **Sie** think the letters stand **für** "Dudes" **und** "Hers."

D *(shtayt)* **steht für** *(dah-men)* **Damen** (ladies)

und **H** **steht für** *(hair-en)* **Herren** (men)**.**

☐ **der Priester** *(pree-stair)*	priest	__________
☐ **das Problem** *(pro-blame)*	problem	__________
☐ **das Programm** *(pro-grahm)*	program	__________
☐ **die Qualität** *(kvah-li-tate)*	quality	__________
☐ **das Restaurant** *(res-tow-rahnt)*	restaurant	__________

Next stop — **das Büro,** specifically **der Tisch oder der Schreibtisch** *(shripe-tish)* desk

in dem Büro. *(bew-roh)* study **Was ist auf** *(owf)* on top of **dem Tisch?** Let's identify **die Dinge** which one normally finds **in dem Büro oder** strewn about **das Haus.**

(bly-shtift) **der Bleistift** pencil	*(koo-lee)* **der Kuli** pen	*(pah-peer)* **das Papier**	*(breef)* **der Brief**
			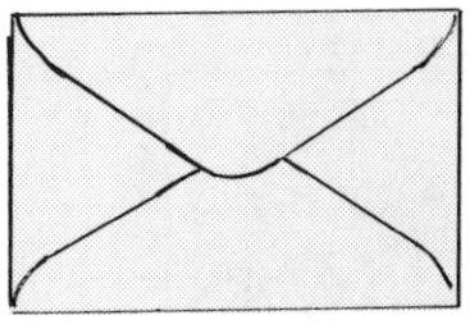
____________	der Kuli	____________	____________
(post-kar-tah) **die Postkarte**	*(breef-mahr-kah)* **die Briefmarke**	*(boohk)* **das Buch**	*(tsight-shrift)* **die Zeitschrift** magazine
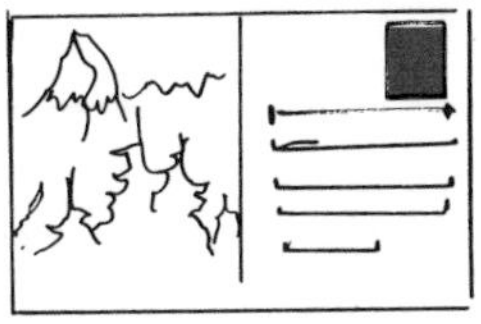			
____________	____________	____________	____________
(tsigh-toong) **die Zeitung** newspaper	*(bril-ah)* **die Brille**	*(fairn-zay-air)* **der Fernseher**	*(pah-peer-kohrp)* **der Papierkorb**

____________	____________	____________	____________

Hier ist ein sehr gutes <u>nicht</u> freies Wort.

☐ **der Quatsch** *(kvaht-sh)* ____________
— This **ist** generally heard in a sentence like **„Das ist Quatsch."** = That is a bunch of baloney.

☐ **das Radio** *(rah-dee-oh)*. . . . . radio ____________

☐ **die Religion** *(ray-lee-gee-ohn)*. . . . . religion ____________

Nun, label these **Dinge in dem Büro** *(bew-roh)* **mit** your stickers. Do not forget to say these **Wörter** out loud whenever **Sie schreiben** *(shry-ben)* (write) them, **Sie** *(zee)* see them, **oder Sie** apply the stickers. **Nun,** identify **die Dinge in dem Bild unten** by filling in each blank **mit dem richtigen** *(reehk-tee-gen)* (correct) **deutschen Wort** *(vort)*.

1. ____________
2. ____________
3. ____________
4. ____________
5. ____________
6. die Postkarte
7. ____________
8. ____________
9. ____________
10. ____________

Hier sind vier *(fear)* **Verben mehr** *(mair)* (more).

sehen *(zeh-en)* = to see

senden *(zen-den)* = to send

schlafen *(shlah-fen)* = to sleep

finden *(fin-den)* = to find

____________ ____________ schlafen ____________

Nun, fill in the blanks, **auf der nächsten** *(nex-sten)* **Seite,** *(zigh-tah)* **mit der richtigen** *(reehk-tee-gen)* form of these **Verben.**

Practice saying the sentences out loud many times.

☐ **die Republik** *(ray-poo-bleek)*.......... republic ____________
☐ **die Residenz** *(ray-zih-dents)*.......... residence ____________
☐ **der Ring** *(ring)*.......................... ring ____________
☐ **das Risiko** *(ree-zee-koh)*............... risk ____________
☐ **rot** *(roht)*............................... red ____________

(zeh-en)
sehen
to see

Ich ______________ **das Bett.**

Er
Sie ______________ **die Bettdecke.**
Es

Wir ______________ **den Wecker.**

Sie (you) ______________ **das Waschbecken.**

Sie (they) sehen **die Dusche.**

(zen-den)
senden
to send

Ich ______________ **den Brief.**

Er
Sie sendet **die Postkarte.**
Es

Wir ______________ **das Buch.**

Sie ______________ **drei Postkarten.**

Sie ______________ **vier Briefe.**

(shlah-fen)
schlafen
to sleep

Ich ______________ **im Schlafzimmer.**

Er
Sie ______________ **im Badezimmer.**
Es

Wir schlafen **im Wohnzimmer.**

Sie ______________ **im Büro.**

Sie ______________ **in der Küche.**

(fin-den)
finden
to find

Ich ______________ **die Briefmarke.**

Er
Sie findet **das Papier.**
Es

Wir ______________ **die Brille.**

Sie ______________ **den Kuli.**

Sie ______________ **die Blumen.**

Remember that **"a"** sounds like "ah." Practice **Land** *(lahnt)*, **schlafen** *(shlah-fen)*, **baden** *(bah-den)*, **danke** *(dahn-kah)*, **was, wann** and **Bank** *(bahnk)*. Also **"au"** is pronounced "ow." Practice **Frau, auf** *(owf)*, **kaufen** *(kow-fen)*, **Haus** *(house)* and **aus** *(ows)*.

Nicht *(neehkt)* means "not" **auf** *(owf)* **Deutsch** *(doych)*. **Nun** *(noon)* practice your pronunciation while **Sie** *(zee)* practice using **"nicht."** Be sure to say the following examples aloud many times.

Das *(dahs)* **ist gut** *(goot)*.
good

Das ist nicht *(neehkt)* **gut.**
not

Heute *(hoy-tah)* **ist Sonntag** *(zohn-tahk)*.
today Sunday

Heute ist nicht *(neehkt)* **Sonntag.**

Das Auto *(ow-toe)* **ist rot** *(roht)*.
red

Das Auto ist nicht rot.

- ☐ **die Ruine** *(roo-ee-nah)*............... ruins ______________
- ☐ **rund** *(roont)*......................... round ______________
- ☐ **das Rußland** *(roos-lahnt))*........... Russia ______________
  — wo sie sprechen Russisch *(roo-sish)* ______________
- ☐ **der Salat** *(zah-laht)*................ salad ______________

Step 15

die Post
mail

(zee) **Sie** know *(noon)* **nun** how to count, how to ask *(frah-gen)* **Fragen,** how to use **Verben mit** the "plug-in" formula, how to make statements, **und** how to describe something, be it the location of a **Hotel oder die Farbe** of a **Haus.** Let's now take the basics that **Sie haben** learned **und** expand them in special areas that will be most helpful in your travels. What does everyone do on a holiday? Send postcards, of course. Let's learn exactly how **das deutsche** *(post-ahmt)* **Postamt** (post office) works.

die Post . . .
nach Amerika
nach Spanien
nach England
nach Italien

Gelb ist die Farbe in Deutschland which identifies *(breef-kah-sten)* **Briefkasten** (mailboxes) **und** *(tay-lay-fohn-tsel-en)* **Telefonzellen.** (telephone booths)

Hier sind the basic *(post-ahmt)* **Postamt-Wörter.** Be sure to practice them out loud **und dann** *(shry-ben)* **schreiben Sie das Wort unter dem Bild.**

der Brief

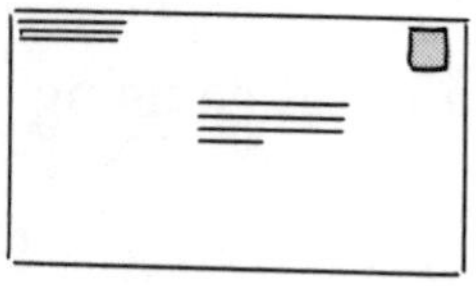

der Brief

die Postkarte

die Briefmarke

(tay-lay-grahm) **das Telegramm**

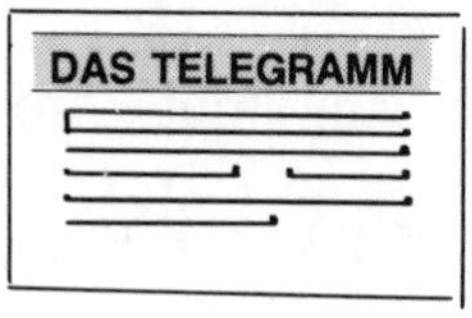

- ☐ **das Salz** *(zahlts)*.................... salt
- ☐ **sauer** *(zow-air)*.................... sour (vs. sweet = **süß)**
- ☐ **scharf** *(sharf)*.................... sharp (spicy)
- ☐ **der Scheck** *(sheck)*.................... check
- ☐ **das Schiff** *(shiff)*.................... ship

das Paket *(pah-kate)*

____

der Briefkasten *(breef-kah-sten)*

____

mit Luftpost *(looft-post)* airmail

____

der Schalter *(shawl-tair)*

____

die Telefonzelle/die Kabine *(tay-lay-fohn-tsel-ah)* *(kah-bee-nah)*

____

das Telefon

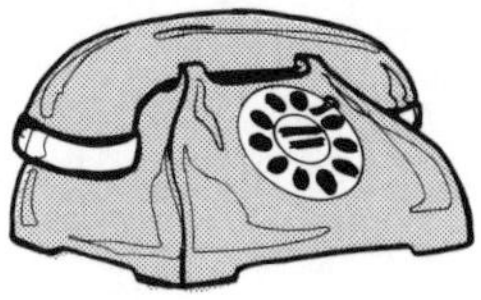

das Telefon

das Postamt

____

Das deutsche Postamt hat alles *(all-es)* (everything)**. Sie senden** *(zen-den)* (send) **Telegramme** (telegrams)**, Briefe** (letters)**, und Postkarten von** *(fohn)* (from) **dem Postamt. Sie kaufen Briefmarken in dem Postamt. Sie machen Telefonanrufe** *(tay-lay-fohn-on-roo-fah)* (telephone calls) **von dem Postamt.** In large cities, **das Postamt hat einen Schalter** *(shawl-tair)* (counter) which is even **auf** (open) **abends** (evenings) **und am Samstag.** If **Sie** *(zee)* need to call home to **Amerika,** this can be done at **das Postamt und heißt** (is called) **ein Ferngespräch** *(fairn-ge-shprake)* (long-distance call)**.** Okay. First step – **Sie gehen** *(gay-en)* **in das Postamt.**

The following **ist eine gute** *(goo-tah)* sample **Konversation.** Familiarize yourself **mit diesen** *(dee-zen)* (these) **Wörtern nun.** Don't wait until your holiday.

- ☐ **die Schokolade** *(show-koh-lah-dah)*. . . . chocolate ______________
- ☐ **das Schottland** *(shoht-lahnt)*. . . . . Scotland ______________
- ☐ **die Schuhe** *(shoo-ah)*. . . . . shoes ______________
- ☐ **die Schule** *(shoo-lah)*. . . . . school ______________
- ☐ **die Schweiz** *(shvites)*. . . . . Switzerland ______________

Next step – **Sie** ask *(frah-gen)* **Fragen** (questions) like those *(oon-ten)* **unten** depending upon *(vahs)* **was Sie** want.

(voh) (kow-fah) **Wo kaufe ich Briefmarken?** (buy)

Wo kaufe ich eine Postkarte?

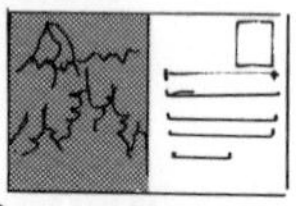

(mah-kah) **Wo mache ich einen Telefonanruf?**

Wo mache ich ein *(fairn-ge-shprake)* **Ferngespräch?**

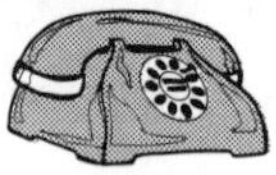

Wo mache ich ein *(orts-ge-shprake)* **Ortsgespräch?** (local call)

(zen-dah) **Wo sende ich ein Telegramm?**

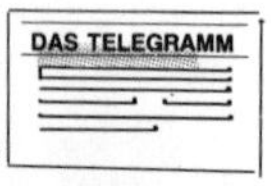

Wo sende ich ein Paket?

Wo ist die Telefonzelle?

(vee-feel) **Wieviel kostet das?**

Wo ist der Postkasten?

Practice these sentences **oben** again and *(vee-dair)* **wieder.** (again)

Nun, quiz yourself. See if **Sie** can translate the following thoughts into **Deutsch.**

Die Antworten sind unten auf der *(nex-sten)* **nächsten** (next) **Seite.**

1. Where is a telephone booth? Wo ist eine Telefonzelle? ____________________
2. Where do I make a phone call? ____________________
3. Where do I make a local phone call? ____________________
4. Where do I make a long-distance phone call? ____________________
5. Where is the post office? ____________________

- ☐ **das Schweden** *(shvay-den)* .... Sweden
  – **wo sie sprechen Schwedisch** *(shvay-dish)*
- ☐ **schwimmen** *(shvim-en)* .... to swim
- ☐ **die See** *(zay)* .... sea
- ☐ **die Sekunde** *(zay-koon-dah)* .... second

6. Where do I buy stamps? ______________________

7. Airmail stamps? ______________________

8. Where do I send a package? ______________________

9. Where do I send a telegram? ______________________

10. Where is counter eight? ______________________

Hier sind mehr Verben.

(mah-ken) **machen** = to make/do *(tsigh-gen)* **zeigen** = to show *(shry-ben)* **schreiben** = to write *(be-tsah-len)* **bezahlen** = to pay

__________ __________ schreiben __________

(mah-ken)
machen
to make/do

Ich __________ einen *(on-roof)* **Anruf** (call).
Er / Sie / Es __________ einen Anruf.
Wir machen viel.

Sie (you) __________ nicht viel.

Sie (they) __________ alles.

(shry-ben)
schreiben
to write

Ich __________ einen Brief.
Er / Sie / Es schreibt viel.
Wir __________ nicht viel.

Sie __________ *(neehk-ts)* **nichts** (nothing).

Sie __________ alles.

(tsigh-gen)
zeigen
to show

Ich __________ *(ee-nen)* **Ihnen** (to you) das Buch.
Er / Sie / Es __________ Ihnen (to you) das Postamt.
Wir __________ Ihnen das *(shloh-ss)* **Schloß** (castle).

Sie __________ mir (to me) das Postamt.

Sie zeigen mir (to me) die Straße.

(be-tsah-len)
bezahlen
to pay

Ich __________ die *(reck-noong)* **Rechnung** (bill).
Er / Sie / Es __________ die Theaterkarten.
Wir __________ die Zugkarten.

Sie bezahlen den Wein.

Sie __________ die Konzertkarten.

ANTWORTEN

1. Wo ist eine Telefonzelle (Kabine)?
2. Wo mache ich einen Telefonanruf?
3. Wo mache ich ein Ortsgespräch?
4. Wo mache ich ein Ferngespräch?
5. Wo ist das Postamt?
6. Wo kaufe ich Briefmarken?
7. Luftpostbriefmarken?
8. Wo sende ich ein Paket?
9. Wo sende ich ein Telegramm?
10. Wo ist Schalter acht?

Step 16

die Quittung (kvi-toong) [receipt] oder die Rechnung (reck-noong) [bill]

Ja, es gibt (gipt) [there are] **auch** bills to pay **in Deutschland. Sie haben** just finished your **(Abendessen)** evening meal **und Sie möchten die Rechnung (bezahlen)** pay. **Was machen Sie? Sie** call for **den Kellner** (kel-nair) [waiter] **oder die Kellnerin** (kel-nair-in) [waitress]:

„Herr Ober!“ (oh-bair) **„Fräulein!“** (froy-line)

Der Kellner will normally reel off what **Sie haben** eaten, while writing rapidly. **Er** will then place **ein kleines** (kline-es) [small] **Stück** (shtewk) [piece] **Papier** (pah-peer) [of paper] **vor** you that looks like **die Rechnung in dem Bild,** while saying something like

„Das macht (mahkt) [makes] **sechsundzwanzig sechzig.“**

Being a seasoned traveler, **Sie** know that tipping as **wir** know **es in Amerika, ist nicht** a custom **in Deutschland**. Generally **die Bedienung** (be-deen-oong) [service] **ist** included **in den** (dain) **Preisen** (pry-zen) [prices]. So, **Sie** pull out **dreißig Mark und,** while placing **das Geld auf den Tisch, Sie sagen,**

Der Kellner then places your **3 DM** change **auf den Tisch und sagt, „Auf Wiedersehen!“**

Sound confusing? **Nein** (nine) [no], just **neu** (noy) [new] **und** different. **Es ist** a custom **in Deutschland,** when paying **in Restaurants,** to round **die Rechnung** (reck-noong) [bill] up to the nearest **Mark oder** half **Mark** according to your preference. So . . .

- ☐ **senden** *(zen-den)* .... to send ____________
- ☐ **der September** *(zep-tem-bair)* .... September ____________
- ☐ **sieben** *(zee-ben)* .... seven ____________
- ☐ **singen** *(zing-en)* .... to sing ____________
- ☐ **sitzen** *(zit-tsen)* .... to sit ____________

25,30 DM becomes 25,50 DM **(fünfundzwanzig Mark fünfzig);**

15,17 DM becomes 15,50 DM **(fünfzehn Mark fünfzig);**

15,55 DM becomes 16,00 DM **(sechzehn Mark).**

See how important numbers are!

This simplifies the system of making change **und** avoids a true tipping situation. Watch **die Leute** *(loy-tah)* people **um** *(oom)* around **Sie in einem Restaurant.** At first **es** seems foreign (which **es ist!**), but **Sie** will catch on quickly **und** your familiarity **mit deutschen** customs will be appreciated.

Hier ist a sample **Konversation** *(kohn-fair-zah-tsi-ohn)* involving paying **die Rechnung** *(reck-noong)* when leaving a **Hotel.**

Karl:	**Entschuldigung** *(ent-shool-dee-goong)*. **Ich möchte die Rechnung** *(reck-noong)* **(die Hotelrechnung) bezahlen.**
Hotelmanager *(hoh-tel-mahn-ah-zhair)*:	**Welches** *(Vel-ches)* Which **Zimmer war** *(vahr)* was **das, bitte?**
Karl:	**Zimmer dreihundertzehn.**
Hotelmanager:	**Danke. Einen** *(ine-in)* **Moment, bitte.**
Hotelmanager:	**Hier ist die Rechnung** *(reck-noong)*. **Das macht neunzig Mark zwanzig.**
Karl:	**Danke (und Karl** hands him **einen Hundertmarkschein. Der Hotelmanager** returns shortly **und sagt)**
Hotelmanager:	**Hier ist Ihre** *(ear-ah)* your **Quittung** *(kvi-toong)* bill **und Ihr** *(ear)* your **Geld (9,80 DM). Danke schön. Auf Wiedersehen!**

Simple, right? If **Sie** ever **haben** any **Probleme** *(pro-blame-ah)* **mit Nummern,** just ask the person to write out **die Nummern** so that **Sie** can be sure you understand everything correctly.

Bitte, schreiben (write) **Sie die Nummern** (numbers) **auf!** (out) **Danke.**

Let's take a break from **Geld und,** starting **auf der nächsten Seite,** learn some **neue** *(noy-ah)* new fun **Wörter.**

- ☐ **der Ski** *(skee)*. . . . . ski ____________
- ☐ **die Socken** *(zoh-ken)*. . . . . socks ____________
- ☐ **der Sommer** *(zoh-mair)*. . . . . summer ____________
- ☐ **die Sonne** *(zoh-nah)*. . . . . sun ____________
- ☐ **die Spezialität** *(shpay-zee-ahl-ih-tate)*. . speciality ____________

(ge-zoont)
Er ist gesund.
healthy

(krahnk)
Er ist krank.
sick

(goot)
Das ist gut.

Das ist nicht gut.
Das ist schlecht.

(hice)
Das Wasser ist heiß.

Es ist 50 Grad.

(kahlt)
Das Wasser ist kalt.

(noor)
Es ist nur 17 Grad.
only

(ly-zah)
Wir sprechen leise.

(laut)
Sie sprechen laut.

(koorts)
Die rote Linie ist kurz.

(lang)
Die blaue Linie ist lang.

Die Frau ist groß.

(kline)
Das Kind ist klein.

Das rote Buch ist dick.

(dewn)
Das grüne Buch ist dünn.

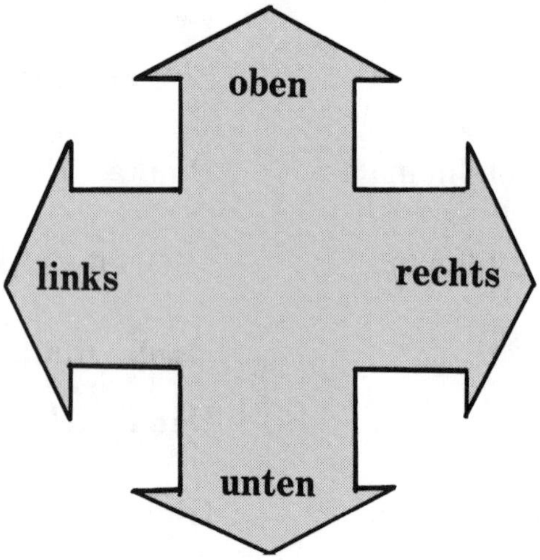

20 Kilometer pro Stunde

(long-zahm)
langsam
slow

200 Kilometer pro Stunde

(shnel)
schnell
fast

- ☐ **das Spanien** *(shpah-nee-en)*........... Spain
  — **wo sie sprechen Spanisch** *(shpah-nish)*
- ☐ **der Sport** *(shport)*.................... sport
- ☐ **der Staat** *(shtaht)*................... state/country
- ☐ **der Student** *(shtoo-dent)*............ student

Die Berge *(bear-gah)* [mountains] sind **hoch** *(hohk)* [high]. Sie sind 2000 Meter hoch.

Die Berge sind **niedrig** *(nee-drig)* [low]. Sie sind nur 800 Meter hoch.

Der Großvater ist **alt** *(ahlt)* [old]. Er ist siebzig Jahre alt.

Das Kind ist **jung** *(yoong)* [young]. Es ist nur zehn Jahre alt.

Das Hotelzimmer ist **teuer** *(toy-air)* [expensive]. Es kostet 94,50 DM.

Das Pensionzimmer ist **billig** *(bil-ig)* [inexpensive]. Es kostet 30,50 DM.

Ich habe 2.000 DM. Ich bin **reich** *(rike)*. Das ist **viel** *(feel)* Geld.

Er hat nur 4 DM. Er ist **arm** *(ahrm)* [poor]. Das ist **wenig** *(vay-nig)* [little] Geld.

Hier sind die neuen Verben.

(viss-en) **wissen** = to know (a fact, an address, etc.)

(kur-nen) **können** = to be able to, can

(mew-sen) **müssen** = to have to, must

(lay-zen) **lesen** = to read

______ ______ ______ lesen

(mew-sen) **Müssen** - *(kur-nen)* **können** - *(viss-en)* **wissen** do not fall neatly into the "plug-in" formula. **Sie sind** actually easier **und sehr** close to **Englisch** in many cases. For **müssen - können - wissen, Sie** only have to learn **zwei** forms for each verb.

(kahn) **kann - können** for **können**

(moos) **muß - müssen** for **müssen**

(vice) **weiß - wissen** for **wissen**

- ☐ **der Sturm** *(shturm)* . . . . storm ______
- ☐ **das Südamerika** *(zewt-ah-mair-ih-kah)* . South America ______
- ☐ **die Suppe** *(zoo-pah)* . . . . soup ______
- ☐ **die Symphonie** *(zewm-foh-nee)* . . . . symphony ______
- ☐ **der Tag** *(tahk)* . . . . day ______

Study their pattern closely as you will use these *(dry)* **drei Verben** a lot.

(kur-nen)
können
to be able to, can

Ich kann **Deutsch lesen.** (can / German / read)
Er / Sie / Es kann **Deutsch sprechen.**
Wir können **Deutsch verstehen.** (can / understand)
Sie können **Englisch verstehen.** (English / understand)
Sie können **Deutsch lesen.** (read)

(mew-sen)
müssen
to have to, must

Ich muß **die Rechnung bezahlen.** (must / the / bill / pay)
Er / Sie / Es muß **die Rechnung bezahlen.**
Wir müssen **die Hotelrechnung bezahlen.** (must / the / hotel bill / pay)
Sie müssen **die Hotelrechnung bezahlen.**
Sie müssen **die Hotelrechnung bezahlen.**

(viss-en)
wissen
to know

Ich weiß **das.**
Er / Sie / Es weiß **das nicht.**
Wir wissen **, wie alt er ist.**
Sie wissen **, wo das Hotel ist.**
Sie wissen **nichts.** (nothing)

(lay-zen)
lesen
to read

Ich ____________ **das Buch.**
Er / Sie / Es ____________ **die** *(tsigh-toong)* **Zeitung.**
Wir lesen **das** *(for-moo-lar)* **Formular.** (form)
Sie (you) ____________ **wenig.**
Sie (they) ____________ **viel.**

Können Sie translate these thoughts **unten** into **Deutsch?** The answers **sind unten.**

1. I can German speak. ____________
2. He must now pay. ____________
3. We know it not. ____________
4. They can the bill pay. ____________
5. She knows a lot. Sie weiß viel.
6. I can a little **(ein bißchen)** German speak. ____________

ANTWORTEN

1. **Ich kann Deutsch sprechen.**
2. **Er muß nun bezahlen.**
3. **Wir wissen es nicht.**
4. **Sie können die Rechnung bezahlen.**
5. **Sie weiß viel.**
6. **Ich kann ein bißchen Deutsch sprechen.**

Nun, draw **Linien** *(lee-nee-en)* between the opposites **unten.** Don't forget to say them out loud. Use these **Wörter** every day to describe **Dinge in Ihrem** *(ear-em)* [your] **Haus, in der Schule** *(shoo-lah)* [school]**,** at work, etc.

groß	**oben**
links	**niedrig**
jung	**klein**
arm	**laut**
gesund	**dünn**
lang	**billig**
viel	**wenig**
gut	**krank**
dick	**alt**
hoch	**schnell**
warm	**rechts**
unten	**kalt**
langsam	**reich**
teuer	**schlecht**
leise	**kurz**

If **Sie** *(zee)* are visiting **Deutschland,** *(doych-lahnt)* **die** *(dee)* **Schweiz** *(shvites)* [Switzerland] **oder Österreich** *(ur-stair-reihk)* [Austria] on a special occasion, **Sie** *(zee)* may want to use one of the following greetings.

Frohe *(froh-ah)* [Merry] **Weihnachten!** *(vie-nahk-ten)* [Christmas]

Schönes *(shurn-es)* [Happy] **Neujahr!** *(noy-yahr)* [New Year]

Ich *(eehk)* **gratuliere!** *(grah-too-lear-ah)* [Congratulations]

ODER

Herzliche *(hairts-leehk-ah)* **Glückswünsche!** *(glewks-veun-shah)* [Congratulations]

Alles *(all-es)* **Gute** *(goo-tah)* **zum** *(tsoom)* **Geburtstag!** *(guh-boorts-tahk)* [Happy Birthday]

Alles Gute zum Jubiläum! *(you-bih-lay-oom)* [Happy Anniversary]

In the following **Wörter**, notice how often **Sie haben ein freies Wort** if **Sie** change the beginning **T** to a **D.**

- ☐ **der Tanz** *(tahnts)*.................. dance ______________________
- ☐ **tanzen** *(tahn-tsen)*.................. to dance ______________________
- ☐ **die Tochter** *(tohk-tair)*.............. daughter ______________________
- ☐ **der Topf** *(tohpf)*.................. pot ______________________

Step 17

Reisen, Reisen, Reisen
(ry-zen) (ry-zen) (ry-zen) — traveling

Gestern nach München! **Heute nach Köln!** **Morgen nach Hamburg!**

Montag in Frankfurt! **Mittwoch in Freiburg!** **Freitag in Nürnberg!**

Traveling **ist** easy, clean, **und sehr** efficient **in Deutschland. Die Bundesrepublik** *(boon-des-ray-poo-bleek)* **Deutschland ist nicht sehr groß. Die Bundesrepublik ist genau** *(ge-now)* exactly **so** *(zoh)* as **groß wie** *(vee)* as **Oregon oder Kolorado und das macht das Reisen sehr einfach** *(ine-fahk)* simple**. Wie reisen Sie durch** *(durhk)* through **Deutschland?**

Hans reist *(ry-st)* travels **mit dem** *(daim)* **Auto.**  **Anita reist mit dem Zug.** 

Helene reist mit dem Flugzeug.  **Hermine reist mit dem Schiff.** 

Karl und Annette reisen mit dem Fahrrad durch Deutschland. 

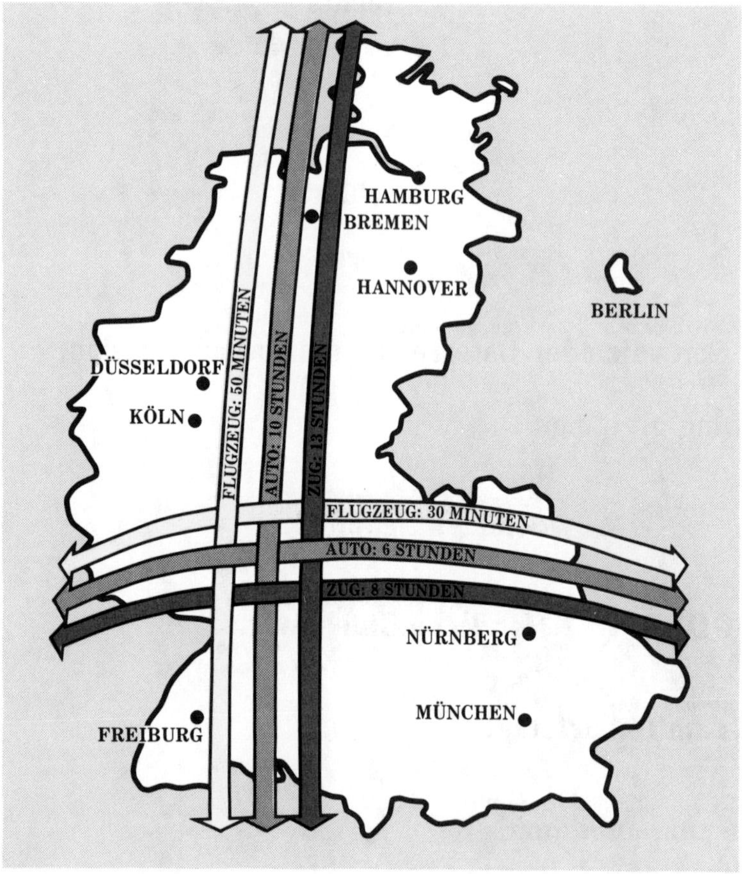

Sehen Sie die Landkarte links? Das ist die Bundesrepublik. Es dauert *(dow-airt)* takes **nur 50 Minuten von Nord nach Süd mit dem Flugzeug, 10 Stunden mit dem Auto, und 13 Stunden mit dem Zug. Gut, nicht** isn't **wahr** *(vahr)* it**? Ja!**

- ☐ **träumen** *(troy-men)* .... to dream ____________
- ☐ **trinken** *(trink-en)* .... to drink ____________
- ☐ **tun** *(toon)* .... to do ____________
- ☐ **die Tür** *(tewr)* .... door ____________
- ☐ **die Uniform** *(oo-nee-form)* .... uniform ____________

Die deutschen Leute *(loy-tah)* [people] love to travel, so **es ist** no surprise to find many **Wörter** built on the **Wort „Reisen“** which can mean either “trip” **oder** “travel.” Practice saying the following **Wörter** many times. **Sie** will see them **oft.**

(ry-zah-ows-koonft) **Reiseauskunft** travel information
(flook-ry-zah) **die Flugreise**
(ow-toh-ry-zah) **die Autoreise**
(tsook-ry-zah) **die Zugreise**
(zay-ry-zah) **die Seereise**
(ry-zah-koh-fair) **der Reisekoffer** trunk
(ry-zah-bew-roh) **das Reisebüro**

Unten sind some basic signs which **Sie** should **auch** learn to recognize quickly. **Gang** *(gong)* comes from the verb **gehen** meaning “to go” **oder** “to walk.” That should help you **mit diesen** *(dee-zen)* [these] **Wörtern.**

(howpt-ine-gong) **der Haupteingang** (main entrance) ____________________

(kine) (ine-gong) **kein Eingang** (no entrance) ____________________

(ine-gong) **der Eingang** (entrance) der Eingang

(ows-gong) **der Ausgang** (exit) ____________________

(howpt-ows-gong) **der Hauptausgang** (main exit) ____________________

(note-ows-gong) **der Notausgang** (emergency exit) ____________________

(ows-gong) **kein Ausgang** (no exit) ____________________

- ☐ **das Ungarn** *(oon-garn)*. . . . . Hungary ____________________
  - **— wo sie sprechen Ungarisch** *(oon-gar-ish)* ____________________
- ☐ **uninteressant** *(oon-in-tair-es-sahnt)* . . . . uninteresting ____________________
- ☐ **die Universität** *(oo-ni-vair-zi-tate)*. . . . . university ____________________
- ☐ **der Untergrund** *(oon-tair-groont)*. . . . . underground (subway) ____________________

(fahr)
Fahr, on the other hand, comes from the verb **fahren** which means "to go by vehicle" **oder** "to drive." These **sind** signs that **Sie** will see on the *(ow-toh-bahn)* **Autobahn** (freeway), plus . . .

(ine-fahrt) **die Einfahrt** ____ entrance for a vehicle	*(ows-fahrt)* **die Ausfahrt** die Ausfahrt exit for a vehicle
die Fahrkarte ____ ticket	**Gute Fahrt!** ____ trip

Hier sind vier sehr *(veehk-tee-guh)* **wichtige** opposites.

Von Frankfurt nach

München und zurück

	Flm ab	ZugNr	an	Bemerkungen		ab	ZugNr	Flman	Bemerkungen
	0.15	D 52	6.05	U Würzburg	C	1.20	E 608	8.16	U Stuttg D Y oG
	1.44	D 364	7.04	Y		6.44	E 783	12.04	(Sa u † oG)
	3.30	D 308	8.46	Y (abWürzbg)					U Würzburg
	7.04	D 30	11.50	✕		7.06	D 465	12.09	✕
B	7.05	F♦ 120	10.48	✕		7.24	TEE 11	11.56	✕ ◇ ☎ U
	7.10	D 312	11.58	✕ U Nürnb E					Mannh ✕ ◇ ☎
	7.23	E 658	12.15	ab Würzb D Y		7.52	D 81	12.13	✕ U Würzb ✕
	8.12	D 245	13.10	✕		8.30	F♦ 33	12.32	✕ ◇ ☎
	8.33	E 692	14.51	U Nürnberg		8.50	D 427	13.34	✕
	8.44	N2628	13.57	U Mhm F♦ ✕ ◇ ☎	B	10.30	D 460	15.12	Y U Stuttgart ✕
Sa	9.21	D2530	14.45	oG Y		11.11	D 267	16.17	✕ U Heidelbg E Y
	9.38	D 530	14.53	✕		12.28	D 83	16.57	✕ U Würzburg ✕
C	9.47	F♦ 38	13.44	✕		12.50	D 257	18.21	Y
	9.55	D 258	14.58	Y		13.04	TEE 21	17.02	✕ ◇ ☎
	10.00	E 560	15.16	U Heidelberg D ✕		13.10	D 481	18.00	Y U Nürnberg ✕
A	10.39	D1314	15.16	✕	Fr	13.51	D2529	18.56	oG Y
	11.01	D 304	15.03	✕ U Würzburg		13.58	D 529	19.10	✕
				TEE ✕ ◇ ☎		14.35	D 383	19.46	✕ U Würzb E
	11.01	D 304	16.04	✕ U Würzbg ✕		14.45	D 403	20.00	✕ U Heidelb ✕ oG

(on-koonft) **die Ankunft** ____ arrival
(ahp-fahrt) **die Abfahrt** ____ departure
(ows-lahnt) **ausland** ausland foreign
(in-lahnt) **inland** ____ domestic

Let's learn the basic travel **Verben.** Follow the same pattern **Sie haben** in previous Steps.

(fahr-en) **fahren** = to drive/travel by vehicle
____

(flee-gen) **fliegen** = to fly
____

(zit-zen) **sitzen** = to sit
____

(booh-ken) **buchen** = to book, as in reserve
____

(lahn-den) **landen** = to land
landen

(on-koh-men) **ankommen** = to arrive
____

(ahp-fahr-en) **abfahren** = to depart
____

(shtai-gen) **steigen** = to climb
____

(oom-shtai-gen) **umsteigen** = to transfer
____

einsteigen = to climb into/board
____

aussteigen = to get out/disembark
____

- ☐ **unten** *(oon-ten)*. . . . . downstairs ____
- ☐ **unter** *(oon-tair)* . . . . under ____
- ☐ **voll** *(fohl)* . . . . full ____
  — ex. **Das Glas ist voll.**
  Der Mann ist voll *(drunk).*

Mit diesen Verben, Sie sind ready for any **Reise** anywhere. Using the "plug-in" formula for **Verben** which **Sie haben** drilled previously, translate the following thoughts into **Deutsch.** The answers **sind unten.**

1. I fly to Frankfurt. Ich fliege nach Frankfurt
2. I drive to Bonn. ______________________
3. We land in Hamburg. ______________________
4. He sits in the airplane. ______________________
5. She books the trip to America. ______________________
6. They travel to Berlin. ______________________
7. Where is the train to Salzburg? ______________________
8. How fly I to England? With Pan Am or with Lufthansa? ______________________

____

Hier sind mehr neue Wörter für die Reise. As always, write out **die Wörter und** practice the sample sentences out loud.

(bahn-hohf)
der Bahnhof
train station

der Bahnhof

Entschuldigung. Wo ist der Bahnhof?

(howpt-bahn-hohf)
der Hauptbahnhof = Hbf
main train station

____

Entschuldigung. Wo ist der Hauptbahnhof?

(flook-hah-fen)
der Flughafen
airport

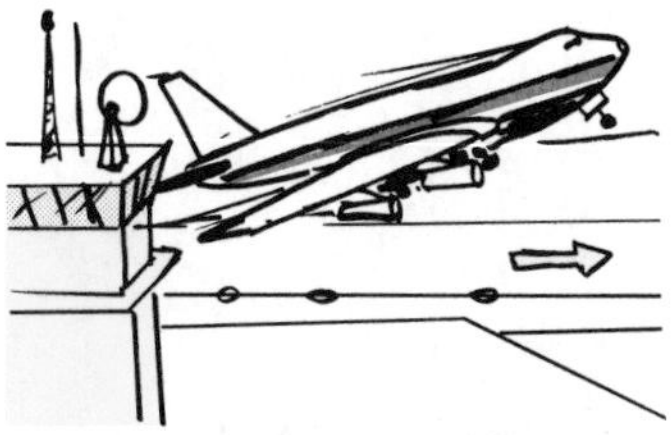

____

Entschuldigung. Wo ist der Flughafen?

ANTWORTEN

1. **Ich fliege nach Frankfurt.**
2. **Ich fahre nach Bonn.**
3. **Wir landen in Hamburg.**
4. **Er sitzt in dem Flugzeug.**
5. **Sie bucht die Reise nach Amerika.**
6. **Sie reisen nach Berlin.**
7. **Wo ist der Zug nach Salzburg?**
8. **Wie fliege ich nach England? Mit Pan Am oder mit Lufthansa?**

(veck-sel-shtoo-bah)
die Wechselstube
money-exchange office

Entschuldigung. Wo ist die Wechselstube?

(foont-bew-roh)
das Fundbüro
lost-and-found office

Entschuldigung. Wo ist das Fundbüro?

(fahr-plahn)
der Fahrplan
timetable/schedule

der Fahrplan

Entschuldigung. Wo ist der Fahrplan?

(be-zetst)
besetzt ____________
occupied

(ahp-tile)
das Abteil das Abteil
compartment

(plahts)
der Platz ____________
seat

Ist dieser Platz besetzt? ____________

Ist dieses Abteil besetzt? ____________

Practice writing out the following (frah-gen) **Fragen.** **Es** will help you (shpay-tair) **später.**
later

Bitte, wo ist die Toilette? ____________

Bitte, wo ist Abteil neun? ____________

Wo ist der (vahr-tah-zahl) **Wartesaal?** Wo ist der Wartesaal?
waiting room

Wo ist Schalter acht? ____________

Ist (rau-ken) **Rauchen** (fair-boh-ten) **verboten?** ____________
smoking, prohibited

☐ **von** *(fohn)* .... from
— ex. **Der Zug kommt von Berlin.**
Die Frau kommt von Gießen.

☐ **vor** *(for)* .... before/in front of
— ex. **Das Kind steht vor dem Hotel.**

Increase your travel **Wörter** by writing out **die Wörter unten und** practicing the sample sentences out loud.

(nahk)
nach ______________________
to
Wo ist der Zug nach Paris?

(tsight)
Zeit ______________________
time
Ich habe wenig Zeit.

(glice)
das Gleis ______________________
track
Der Zug fährt vom Gleis 7 ab.

(bahn-shtike)
der Bahnsteig der Bahnsteig
platform
Der Zug kommt auf Bahnsteig 8 an.

Practice these **Wörter** every day. **Sie** will be surprised **wie oft Sie** will use them. **Können Sie** the following *(lay-zen)* **lesen?** (read)

> **Sie sitzen nun im Flugzeug und Sie** *(flee-gen)* **fliegen nach Deutschland. Sie haben Geld** exchanged (you have, haven't you?), **Sie haben die Fahrkarten und den Paß, und Sie haben den Reisekoffer** packed. **Sie sind nun Tourist. Sie** *(lahn-den)* **landen morgen um 14:15 in Deutschland. Gute Reise!** *(feel)* **Viel** *(shpahss)* **Spaß!**

Nun, Sie have arrived **und Sie** head for the *(bahn-hohf)* **Bahnhof** in order to get to your final destination. **Deutsche** *(tsew-gah)* **Züge** (trains) come in many shapes, sizes, **und** speeds. **Es** *(gipt)* **gibt** (there are) *(pair-zoh-nen-tsew-gah)* **Personenzüge (sehr langsam)**, *(ile-tsew-gah)* **Eilzüge (langsam)**, *(shnel-tsew-gah)* **Schnellzüge (schnell), und** *(in-tair)* **Inter-City** *(tsew-gah)* **Züge (sehr schnell).** Some **Züge haben einen** *(shpy-zah-vah-gen)* **Speisewagen** (dining car) **und some Züge haben einen Schlafwagen** (sleeping car) **oder einen** *(lee-gah-vah-gen)* **Liegewagen** (car with berths)**.** All this will be indicated on the **Zugfahrplan,** but remember, **Sie wissen auch** how to ask **Dinge** like this. Practice your possible **Frage** combinations by writing out the following samples.

Hat der Zug einen *(shpy-zah-vah-gen)* **Speisewagen?** Hat der Zug einen Speisewagen?

Hat der Zug einen *(lee-gah-vah-gen)* **Liegewagen?** ______________________

Hat der Zug einen *(shlahf-vah-gen)* **Schlafwagen?** ______________________

- ☐ **das Volk** *(folk)*.................... folk/people ____________
- ☐ **der Vater** *(fah-tair)*.................. father ____________
  — ex. **Der Vater heißt Herr Taler.** ____________
- ☐ **der Vorname** *(for-nah-mah)*.......... first name ____________
  — ex. **Der Vater heißt Helmut mit Vorname.** ____________

What about inquiring about **Preisen?** **Sie** *(kur-nen)* **können das auch fragen.**

(vahs) **Was** **kostet** *(dee)* **die Fahrt nach** *(high-del-bairg)* **Heidelberg?** ____________________

(ine-fahk) **einfach** (one-way) einfach ____________________ **hin und** *(tsoo-rewk)* **zurück** (there and back (round-trip)) ____________________

Was kostet die Fahrt nach *(veen)* **Wien?** (Vienna) ____________________

Was kostet die Fahrt nach *(koh-pen-hah-gen)* **Kopenhagen?** ____________________

Einfach oder hin und zurück? ____________________

What about *(ahp-fahrt)* **Abfahrt** (departure) **und** *(on-koonft)* **Ankunft** (arrival) times? **Sie** *(kur-nen)* **können das auch fragen!**

(vahn) **Wann** *(gate)* **geht der Zug nach** *(mahr-burg)* **Marburg?** Wann geht der Zug nach Marburg?

Wann geht der *(flook)* **Flug nach** *(rohm)* **Rom?** ____________________

Wann kommt der *(tsook)* **Zug aus** *(mah-drid)* **Madrid?** ____________________

Wann kommt der Flug aus *(bear-leen)* **Berlin?** ____________________

Sie have arrived **in Deutschland.** **Sie sind nun** *(ahm)* **am** (at the) **Bahnhof.** **Wo** do **Sie** want to go? Well, tell that to the person at the **Schalter** selling **Karten!**

Ich *(murk-tah)* **möchte nach** *(dort-moont)* **Dortmund fahren.** (to travel) ____________________

Ich möchte nach *(lew-beck)* **Lübeck fahren.** ____________________

Wir möchten nach Innsbruck fahren. ____________________

(vahn) **Wann geht der Zug nach Innsbruck?** ____________________

(vahs) **Was kostet eine Karte nach Innsbruck?** ____________________

Ich möchte eine Karte nach Innsbruck. ____________________

(air-sta) **erste** (first) *(klah-sah)* **Klasse** (class) erste Klasse ____________________ *(tsvai-tah)* **zweite** (second) *(klah-sah)* **Klasse** (class) ____________________

Einfach oder hin und zurück? ____________________

(moos) **Muß ich** *(oom-shtai-gen)* **umsteigen?** ____________________ *(dahn-kah)* **Danke.** ____________________

Mit this practice, **Sie sind** off **und** running. **Diese Reisewörter** will make your holiday twice as enjoyable **und** at least three times as easy. Review **diese neuen Wörter** by doing the crossword puzzle **auf Seite** 77. Practice drilling yourself on this Step by selecting other locations **und** asking your own **Fragen** about **Züge, Busse** *(boos-sah)*, **oder Flugzeuge** *(flook-tsoy-gah)* that go there. Select **neue Wörter** from your **Wörterbuch und** practice asking questions that

beginnen mit **WO** **WANN** **WAS KOSTET** **WIE OFT**

oder making statements like **Ich möchte nach Hamburg fahren. Ich möchte eine Karte kaufen.**

ACROSS
1. restaurant
2. to drive, go to
3. train
4. money
5. sleeping car
6. entrance
7. free, available
8. nothing
9. I
10. yes
11. exit (for cars)
12. exit (for people)
13. to fly
14. ticket
15. trip
16. no
17. train trip

DOWN
1. smoker
2. airport
10. yes
19. time
20. suitcase
21. simple/one way
22. travel info
23. to
24. with
25. train station
26. foreign
27. non-smoker
28. passport
29. ocean voyage
30. occupied
31. she
32. he
33. domestic

ANTWORTEN ZUM KREUZWORTRÄTSEL

ACROSS
1. **Restaurant**
2. **fahren**
3. **Zug**
4. **Geld**
5. **Schlafwagen**
6. **Eingang**
7. **frei**
8. **nichts**
9. **ich**
10. **ja**
11. **Ausfahrt**
12. **Ausgang**
13. **fliegen**
14. **Fahrkarte**
15. **Reise**
16. **nein**
17. **Zugreise**

DOWN
1. **Raucher**
2. **Flughafen**
10. **ja**
19. **Zeit**
20. **Koffer**
21. **einfach**
22. **Reiseauskunft**
23. **nach**
24. **mit**
25. **Bahnhof**
26. **ausland**
27. **Nichtraucher**
28. **Pass**
29. **Seereise**
30. **besetzt**
31. **sie**
32. **er**
33. **inland**

Step 18

(shpy-zah-kar-tah)
die Speisekarte
menu

Sie sind nun in Deutschland und Sie haben ein Hotelzimmer. Und nun? Sie sind hungrig (hoon-grig) (hungry). **Sie möchten essen. Wo ist ein gutes** (goo-tes) **Restaurant?** First of all, **es gibt** (gipt) (there are) different types of places to eat. Let's learn them.

das Gasthaus (gahst-house)**/der Gasthof** (gahst-hohf)	=	an inn with a full range of meals
das Café (kah-fay)	=	a coffee shop with pastries, snacks **und** beverages (This should be a regular stop every day about 3:30 p.m.)
der Schnellimbiß (shnel-im-biss)	=	a snack bar, usually specializing in **Wurst** (vurst) (sausages) **und** beverages
das Restaurant	=	exactly what it says, with a variety of meals
die Weinstube (vine-shtoo-bah)	=	a small, cozy restaurant specializing in **Weine** with some hot dishes, cheeses, **und** snacks
die Bierhalle (beer-hahl-ah)	=	besides **Bier, Sie können auch** hot dishes, **Wurst**, pretzels **und Salate** (zah-lah-tah) **bestellen**
der Ratskeller (rahts-kel-lair)	=	a type of restaurant frequently found in the basement of **das Rathaus** (raht-house) (city hall)

Try all of them. Experiment. **Sie finden nun ein gutes Restaurant. Sie gehen in das Restaurant und Sie finden einen Platz** (plahts). Sharing **Tische** (tables) **mit** others **ist** a common **und sehr** pleasant custom **in Europa.** If **Sie sehen** (zay-en) a vacant **Stuhl** (shtool), just be sure to first ask

(ent-shool-dee-goong) (fry)
Entschuldigung. Ist dieser Platz frei?

If **Sie brauchen** (brow-ken) (need) **eine Speisekarte**, catch the attention of the **Kellner und** say

Herr Ober! Die Speisekarte, bitte.

☐ **die Vereinigten Staaten** *(fair-eye-neehk-ten shtah-ten)*. . United States
— ex. **Ich wohne in den Vereinigten Staaten.**
Ich komme aus den Vereinigten Staaten.
Ich arbeite in den Vereinigten Staaten.
Ich reise in den Vereinigten Staaten.

In Deutschland, es gibt drei main meals to enjoy every day, plus **Kaffee** *(kah-fay)* **und Kuchen** *(koo-khen)* (pastry) in the **späten Nachmittag.**

das Frühstück *(frew-shtewk)*	= breakfast	**in Hotels und Pensionen** *(pawn-tsi-oh-nen)* this meal may start as early as 6:00 **und** finish at 8:00. Be sure to check the schedule before you retire for the night.
das Mittagessen *(mit-tahk-es-sen)* (midday meal)	= lunch	generally served from 11:30 to 14:00. For most people, this **ist** the main meal of the day.
das Abendessen *(ah-bent-es-sen)*	= dinner	generally served from 18:00 to 20:30 and sometimes later; frequently after 21:30, only cold snacks **oder heiße** (hot) **Wurst** are served in **Restaurants.**

If **Sie** look around you **in einem Restaurant, Sie** will see that some **deutsche Tisch** customs **sind** different from ours. For example, **Kartoffeln sind** never cut **mit einem Messer.** Before starting **das Essen, Sie** always wish **die Leute** in your party **oder** those sharing your **Tisch** **„Guten Appetit."** Before clearing the dishes, **der Kellner** will ask, **„Hat's geschmeckt?"** **Er** is asking if **Sie** enjoyed your **Essen und** if it tasted good. A smile **und** a **„Ja, danke"** will tell him that you enjoyed it.

Nun, it may be **Frühstück** *(frew-shtewk)* time **in Denver**, but **Sie sind in Deutschland und es ist 18 Uhr.** Most **deutsche Restaurants** post **die Speisekarte** outside. Always read it before entering so **Sie wissen** *(viss-en)* what type of meals **und Preisen** *(pry-zen)* (prices) **Sie** will encounter inside. Most **Restaurants** offer **ein Menü** *(men-ew)* **oder ein Tagesgericht** *(tah-ges-ge-reehkt)* (special meal of the day). This is a complete meal at a fair **Preis** *(price)*. In addition, **es gibt** all the following main categories **auf der Speisekarte.**

- ☐ **das Wasser** *(vah-sair)*............... water ______________
- ☐ **der Westen** *(ves-ten)*............... West ______________
- ☐ **das Wild** *(vilt)*..................... venison ______________
- ☐ **der Wein** *(vine)*..................... wine ______________
- ☐ **der Wind** *(vint)*..................... wind ______________

(for-shpy-zen)
Vorspeisen . . . . hors d'oeuvres

(zoo-pen)
Suppen . . . . soups

(eye-air-shpy-zen)
Eierspeisen . . . . egg dishes

Toast . . . . toast dishes

(fish-ge-reehk-tah)
Fischgerichte . . . . fish dishes

(fair-tee-gah)(ge-reehk-tah)
Fertige Gerichte . . . . entrees

(fahn-en-ge-reehk-tah)
Grill- und Pfannengerichte . . . . grilled and fried food

(pair-zohn-en)
Für 2 Personen . . . . meals for two people

(kahl-tah) (shpy-zen)
Kalte Speisen . . . . cold meals (plates of cheese and cold cuts)

(nahk-shpy-zen)
Nachspeisen
Nachtisch . . . . dessert

Most **Restaurants** also offer **Spezialitäten** *(shpay-tsee-ahl-ih-tate-en)* (specialties) **des Hauses oder** specific meals prepared **nach Art des Hauses** (according to the chef's style). If **Sie** happen to be traveling **mit Kindern**, look for the **Kinderteller** *(kin-dair-tell-air)* (children's plate). **Nun** for a preview of delights to come . . . At the back of this **Buch Sie finden eine** sample **deutsche Speisekarte. Lesen** *(lay-zen)* (read) **Sie die Speisekarte heute und lernen Sie die neuen Wörter!** When **Sie** are ready to leave for **Europa**, *(oy-roh-pah)* cut out **die Speisekarte**, *(shpy-zah-kar-tah)* fold it **und** carry it in your pocket, wallet, **oder** purse. **Sie** can **nun** go in any **Restaurant und** feel prepared! (May I suggest studying **die Speisekarte** before **und** not after **Sie haben** eaten!)

☐ **der Winter** *(vin-tair)*	winter	____________
☐ **die Wolle** *(voh-lah)*	wool	____________
☐ **Willkommen!** *(vill-koh-men)*	Welcome!	____________
☐ **wandern** *(vahn-dairn)*	to wander	____________
☐ **die Waren** *(vahr-en)*	wares	____________

In addition, learning the following should help you to identify what kind of meat **oder** poultry **Sie bestellen** (order) **und wie** *(vee)* **es** will be prepared.

vom Rind *(rint)* beef

vom Kalb *(kahlp)* veal

vom Schwein *(shvine)* pork

vom Hammel *(hah-mel)* mutton

Geflügel *(ge-flew-gel)* poultry

Wild *(vilt)* venison

gekocht *(ge-kohkt)* = cooked

gebraten *(ge-brah-ten)* = roasted/fried

gebacken *(ge-bah-ken)* = baked

paniert *(pahn-ear-t)* = breaded

gegrillt *(ge-grilt)* = grilled

im Backteig *(bahk-taig)* = in batter

Sie will also get **Gemüse** *(ge-mew-zah)* (vegetables) **und Kartoffeln** *(kahr-toh-feln)* (potatoes) **mit** your **Essen und einen gemischten** *(ge-mish-ten)* (mixed) **Salat.** One day at an open-air **Markt** (market) will teach you **die Namen** for all the different kinds of **Gemüse und Obst** *(ohpst)* (fruit)**,** plus it will be a delightful experience for you. **Sie können** always consult your menu guide at the back of this **Buch** if **Sie vergessen** *(fair-gess-en)* (forget) **den richtigen Namen. Nun Sie haben** decided **was Sie möchten essen und der Kellner kommt.**

- ☐ **warm** *(varm)* .... warm ______________
- ☐ **die Warnung** *(vahr-noong)* .... warning ______________
- ☐ **wünschen** *(vewn-shen)* .... to wish ______________
  — ex. **Was wünschen Sie?** ______________
- ☐ **der Weg** *(veg)* .... way ______________

Don't forget about treating yourself to a **Nachtisch oder Nachspeise.** You would **nicht** want to miss out on trying the following desserts.

(ge-mish-tes) (ice)
Gemischtes Eis
two or three scoops of ice cream

(ice-beck-air) (frewk-ten)
Eisbecher mit Früchten
an ice-cream cup **mit** fruit, liqueur **und** whipped cream

(zah-nah)
Gemischtes Eis mit Sahne
two or three scoops of ice cream **mit** whipped cream

(dahm) (blahnsh)
Dame Blanche
Vanilleeis mit hot chocolate sauce

After completing your **Essen** (meal), call **den Kellner und** pay just as **Sie haben** already learned in Step 16:

Herr Ober, ich möchte zahlen.

Unten ist a sample **Speisekarte** to help you prepare for your holiday.

RESTAURANT ZUM GOLDENEN HIRSCHEN

SPEISEKARTE

VORSPEISEN

Nordseekrabben-Cocktail (North Sea shrimp cocktail) .... DM 7,00
Matjeshering in saurer Sahne (pickled herring in sour cream) .. 6,00
Geräucherte Lachsschnitten garniert (smoked salmon) 9,50
Westfälischer Schinken mit Bauernbrot (Westphalian ham with rye bread) 10,00
Gefüllte Eier (deviled eggs) 4,00

SUPPEN

Fleischbrühe mit Ei (clear broth with egg) 2,75
Hühnerbrühe mit Reis (chicken broth with rice) 3,25
Ochsenschwanzsuppe (oxtail soup) 4,00

HAUPTGERICHTE

Filet Mignon mit pommes frites und Spargel (filet mignon with French fries, asparagus) 16,50
Bachforelle blau mit Petersilienkartoffeln und Gurkensalat (blue brook trout with parsley potatoes, cucumber salad) 14,50
Wiener Schnitzel mit Röstkartoffeln und Erbsen (breaded veal cutlet with roasted potatoes, peas) 11,80
Kasseler Rippchen mit Sauerkraut und Kartoffelpüree (smoked pork chops, sauerkraut, mashed potatoes) 9,00
Ungarisches Gulasch mit Butternudeln und gemischten Salat (Hungarian goulash with buttered noodles, mixed salad) 8,50
Sauerbraten mit Rotkraut und Klößen (sauerbraten with red cabbage, dumplings) 12,00
Rehragout mit Pilzen, Eierspätzle und Preiselbeeren (ragout of venison with mushrooms, homemade egg noodles, cranberries) 11,50
Gänsebraten mit Weinkraut und Kartoffelpüree (roasted goose with wine cabbage, mashed potatoes) 15,25
Hühnerfrikassee mit Reis, Bohnen und gemischtem Salat (chicken stew with rice, green beans, mixed salad) 8,50
Gebratenes 1/2 Huhn mit Kartoffelsalat (roasted chicken with potato salad) 8,25
Jägerschnitzel 12,75

NACHSPEISEN

Gemischtes Eis mit Schlagsahne 3,00
Apfelstrudel (apple strudel) 2,90
Käsekuchen (cheese cake) 2,90
Obsttorte (fruit pastry) 2,75
Gemischte Käseplatte mit Brot und Butter (assorted cheeses with bread and butter) 7,50

GETRÄNKE

Weißweine ...... 10,50—31,00
Rotweine 10,50-31,00
Liköre, Weinbrände (liqueurs and brandies) 3,50
Bier 2,25-4,50
Mineralwasser 2,25
Fruchtsäfte (fruit juices) 2,25
Kaffee 2,50-4,00
Tee 3,00

Unsere Preise sind Endpreise einschließlich Bedienungsgeld und Mehrwertsteuer. (Our prices include service and sales tax.)

☐ **der Zentimeter** *(tsen-tih-may-tair)*.... centimeter ______
☐ **das Zentrum** *(tsen-troom)*........... center ______
☐ **die Zeremonie** *(tsair-ih-moh-nee)*...... ceremony ______
☐ **die Zigarette** *(tsih-gah-ret-tah)*........ cigarette ______
☐ **die Zigarre** *(tsih-gah-rah)*............ cigar ______

Frühstück ist ein bißchen different because **es ist** fairly standardized **und Sie** will frequently take it at your **Pension** *(pawn-tsi-ohn)* as **es ist** included **in dem Preis** of the **Zimmer. Unten ist** a sample of what **Sie können** expect to greet you **am Morgen** (in the morning).

Frühstück 1 . . . . DM 3,45

1 Tasse Kaffee, Tee oder Schokolade
Brot und Brötchen, Butter,
Marmelade und 1 gekochtes Ei

Frühstück 2 . . . . DM 4,20

1 Portion Kaffee, Tee oder Kakao
1 Glas Orangensaft
2 Brötchen, versch. belegt (assorted toppings)

Frühstück 3 . . . . DM 4,50

1 Kännchen Kaffee, Tee oder Schokolade
Butter, Brot und Brötchen
dazu 1 kleine Aufschnittplatte (plate of cold cuts)

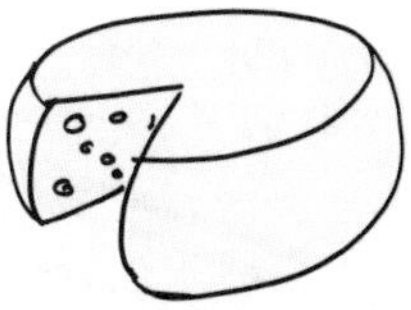

Beilagen zum Frühstück

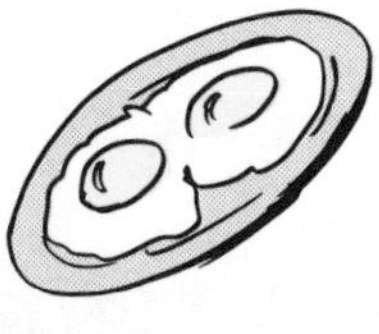

1 frisch gekochtes Ei . . . . DM 0,75
Frühstücksportion Holländer Käse . . . . DM 2,00
Frühstücksportion gekochter Schinken . . . . . DM 2,60
Frühstücksportion gemischter Aufschnitt . . . DM 3,50

☐ **der Zirkus** *(tsir-koos)* . . . . circus ________________
☐ **die Zivilisation** *(tsih-vih-lih-zah-tsi-ohn)* . . . . . civilization ________________
☐ **der Zoo** *(tsoh)* . . . . zoo ________________
☐ **zu** *(tsoo)* . . . . to ________________
☐ **der Zucker** *(tsoo-kair)* . . . . sugar ________________

Step 19

das Telefon *(tay-lay-fohn)* telephone

Was *(vahs)* **ist** different about **das Telefon in Deutschland**? Well, **Sie** never notice such things until **Sie** want to use them. **Telefone** allow you to reserve **Hotelzimmer** in another **Stadt** *(shtaht)* city, call friends, reserve **Theaterkarten** *(tay-ah-tair-kar-ten)*, **Konzertkarten**, **oder Ballettkarten**, make emergency calls, check on the hours of a **Museum** *(moo-zay-oom)*, rent **ein Auto**, **und** all those other **Dinge** which **wir machen** on a daily basis. **Es** also gives you a certain amount of freedom — **Sie können** your own calls **machen**.

Having **ein Telefon in Ihrem** *(ear-em)* **Haus ist nicht** as common **in Deutschland** as **in Amerika**. That means **Sie können Telefonzellen** *(tay-lay-fohn-tsel-en)* everywhere **finden**. Since they **sind** state-owned, **sie** *they* sport **die Farbe gelb** just like **die Postkasten.**

Das ist eine deutsche Telefonzelle.

So far, so good. **Nun** let's read the instructions for using **das Telefon.** This **ist** one of those moments when you realize,

Ich bin nicht in Amerika.

So let's learn how to operate **das Telefon.**

This **ist** your first encounter with what **ist** known as **Amtsdeutsch** *(ahmts-doych)* (bureaucratic German). All **es ist, ist** complicated **Wörter für einfache** *(ine-fahk-ah)* (simple) **Wörter.** Some of these **Wörter** you should be able to recognize already. Let's learn the others. Stick to the **Deutsch und Sie** will be fine!

ÖFFENTLICHER MÜNZFERNSPRECHER

Orts- und Ferngespräche

Keine (no) **Telegramme, keine** (no) **Auslandsgespräche**

Handapparat (receiver) **abnehmen** (lift)

Wahlton (dial tone) **abwarten** (wait for)

Mindestens (at least) **20 Pfennig einwerfen** (throw in)

Wählen (dial)

Bei (with) **Ferngesprächen** (long-distance calls) **Vorwahlnummer** (area code) **nicht** (not) **vergessen** (forget)

Nach (after) **beendetem** (completed) **Gespräch** (call)

Handapparat (receiver) **einhängen** (hang up)

Überfall (accident), **Verkehrsunfall** (traffic accident) ________ **110**

Feuer (fire) ________ **112**

Rettungsdienst (rescue service) ________ **112**

Auskunft (information) ________ **118**

Englisch		Deutsch		Amtsdeutsch
the telephone	=	**das Telefon**	=	**der Fernsprecher** **der öffentliche Fernsprecher**
the coin telephone	=	**das Telefon**	=	**der Münzfernsprecher** **der öffentliche Münzfernsprecher**
the telephone booth	=	**die Telefonzelle**	=	**die Fernsprechzelle** **die öffentliche Fernsprechzelle**
the telephone book	=	**das Telefonbuch**	=	**das Fernsprechverzeichnis**
the telephone conversation	=	**das Telefongespräch**	=	**das Ferngespräch** **das Ortsgespräch**
to telephone / call	=	**telefonieren**	=	**anrufen**

So **nun Sie haben** the simple **und** the complicated versions of **das Telefon. Es gibt** area codes **in Deutschland** just as **in Amerika und sie heißen „die Vorwahlnummer."** (for-vahl-noo-mair) A large **Stadt** (shtaht) city like **Frankfurt oder München hat eine Vorwahlnummer** like 060 **oder** 080. Then a portion of the large **Stadt** might have **eine Vorwahlnummer** like 061 **oder** 082. A smaller suburb might be 0613 **oder** 0824, **und** finally, a small town farther away would have **eine Vorwahlnummer** like 06139 **oder** 08241. So just through **die Vorwahlnummer lernen Sie ein bißchen** about the size of the town **Sie telefonieren und** its proximity to a major **Stadt.**

When answering **das Telefon, Sie** pick up **den Handapparat** (hahnt-ah-pah-raht) receiver **und** just say your **Name,** (nah-mah) „Elke Schmidt." When saying good-bye, **Sie sagen, „Auf Wiederhören"** (owf) (vee-dair-hur-en) hear from you again — *not* **„Auf Wiedersehen."** (vee-dair-zay-en) see you again **Hier sind** some sample possibilities **für ein Telefongespräch** (tay-lay-fohn-ge-shprake). Write them in the blanks **unten.**

Ich möchte Auto Firma Schmidt anrufen. (ow-toh) (fear-mah) (on-roo-fen) ____________________

Ich möchte Chikago anrufen. Ich möchte Chikago anrufen.

Ich möchte Frau Liebsch in Heidelberg anrufen. (leebsh) ____________________

Ich möchte Lufthansa in Frankfurt anrufen. (looft-hahn-za) ____________________

Ich möchte ein R-gespräch machen. (air-ge-shprake) collect call ____________________

Wo ist eine Telefonzelle? ____________________

Wo ist das Telefonbuch? ____________________

Meine Nummer ist 67598. (my-nah) my ____________________

Was ist die Telefonnummer? ____________________

 Hier ist another possible **Konversation.** Listen to the **Wörter und wie sie** are used.

Thomas: **Hallo, hier ist Herr Faber. Ich möchte mit Frau Schirer** *(shy-rair)* **sprechen.**

Sekretärin *(zeh-kre-tear-in)*: **Einen** (one) **Augenblick** *(ow-gen-bleek)* (moment). **Ich verbinde** *(fair-bin-dah)* (connect). **Es tut** *(toot)* **mir leid** *(light)* (I'm sorry). **Es ist besetzt.**

Thomas: **Wiederholen** *(vee-dair-hoh-len)* **Sie das bitte. Ich spreche nur ein bißchen Deutsch.**

Sprechen Sie bitte langsamer *(long-zah-mair)* (slower).

Sekretärin: **Es tut mir leid. Es ist besetzt.**

Thomas: **Ah. Danke. Auf Wiederhören** *(vee-dair-hur-en)*.

Und noch *(nohk)* (still) **eine** possibility . . .

Christina: **Ich möchte Auskunft** *(ows-koonft)* (information) **für Kassel, bitte. Ich möchte die Telefonnummer für Herrn** *(hairn)* (Mr.) **Doktor** (Dr.) **Friedrich Bopp, bitte.**

Auskunft: **Die Nummer ist 0881-5552.**

Christina: **Wiederholen** *(vee-dair-hoh-len)* **Sie das, bitte.**

Auskunft: **Die Nummer ist 0881-5552.**

Christina: **Danke. Auf Wiederhören.**

Sie sind nun ready to use any **Telefon in Deutschland**. Just take it **langsam und** speak clearly.

Don't forget that **Sie können fragen . . .**

Was kostet ein Ortsgespräch *(orts-ge-shprake)***?**

Was kostet ein Ortsgespräch?

____

Was kostet ein Telefongespräch nach Amerika?

____

Was kostet ein Ferngespräch *(fairn-ge-shprake)* **nach Bremen?**

____

Was kostet ein Ferngespräch nach Italien?

____

Don't forget that **Sie brauchen Kleingeld** *(kline-gelt)* **für das Telefon!**

Step 20

(oo-bahn)
die U-Bahn
subway

(oo-bahn) **„U-Bahn"** **ist der deutsche Name für** the subway. **Die großen** (large) (shtay-tah) **Städte** (cities) **in Deutschland haben eine U-Bahn** just like **die großen** (shtay-tah) **Städte in Amerika. Sie** will find **eine U-Bahn in den großen Städten** like (bohn) **Bonn,** (hahm-boorg) **Hamburg,** (bear-leen) **Berlin (Ost und West),** (frahnk-furt) **Frankfurt und** (mewn-shen) **München. Die kleineren Städte** like (high-del-bairg) **Heidelberg,** (mahn-hime) **Mannheim, und** (fry-boorg) **Freiburg haben eine** (shtrah-sen-bahn) **Straßenbahn,** or what we call a streetcar. Both **die U-Bahn und die** (shtrah-sen-bahn) **Straßenbahn (S-Bahn) sind** (ine-fahk) **einfach** (simple) **und** quick ways to travel. (vel-chah) **Welche** (which) **Wörter** (mew-sen) **müssen** (must) **Sie für die U-Bahn und die Straßenbahn** (viss-en) **wissen** (know)? Let's learn them by practicing them aloud **und dann** by writing them in the blanks **unten.**

(dee) (oo-bahn) **die U-Bahn**

____

(shtrah-sen-bahn) **die Straßenbahn**

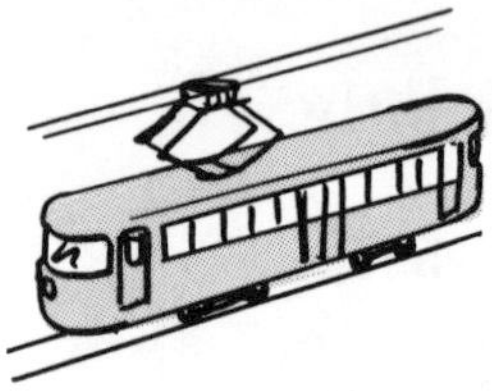

____

(boos) **der Bus**

der Bus

(hahl-tah-shtel-ah) **die Haltestelle** = the stop ____________________

(lee-nee-ah) **die Linie** = the line die Linie

(shahf-nair) **der Schaffner** = the conductor ____________________

Let's also review the "transportation" **Verben** at this point.

(ine-shtai-gen) **einsteigen** = to get in/board

____

(ows-shtai-gen) **aussteigen** = to get out/disembark

aussteigen

(oom-shtai-gen) **umsteigen** = to transfer

____

(ine-shtem-peln) **einstempeln** = to have a ticket stamped

____

Maps displaying the various **Linien** *(lee-nee-en)* **und Haltestellen** *(hahl-tah-shtel-en)* [stops] **sind** generally posted outside every **Eingang** *(ine-gong)* **für die U-Bahn**. Normally **der U-Bahnfahrplan** *(oo-bahn-fahr-plahn)* [subway schedule] **ist** available at a **Fremdenverkehrsamt,** *(frem-den-fair-kairs-ahmt)* [tourist information office] possibly a **Reisebüro, oder** even a **Kiosk** *(key-ohsk)* [newsstand]. Just as **in Amerika, die Linien sind** frequently color-coded to make the **Fahrplan** [schedule] **sehr einfach** to **verstehen** *(fair-shtay-en)*. Other than having foreign **Wörter, deutsche U-Bahnen sind** just like **amerikanische U-Bahnen.** Check the **Name** of the last **Haltestelle** on the **Linie** which you should take **und** catch the **U-Bahn** traveling in that direction. The same applies for the **Straßenbahn**. See the **Fahrplan unten.**

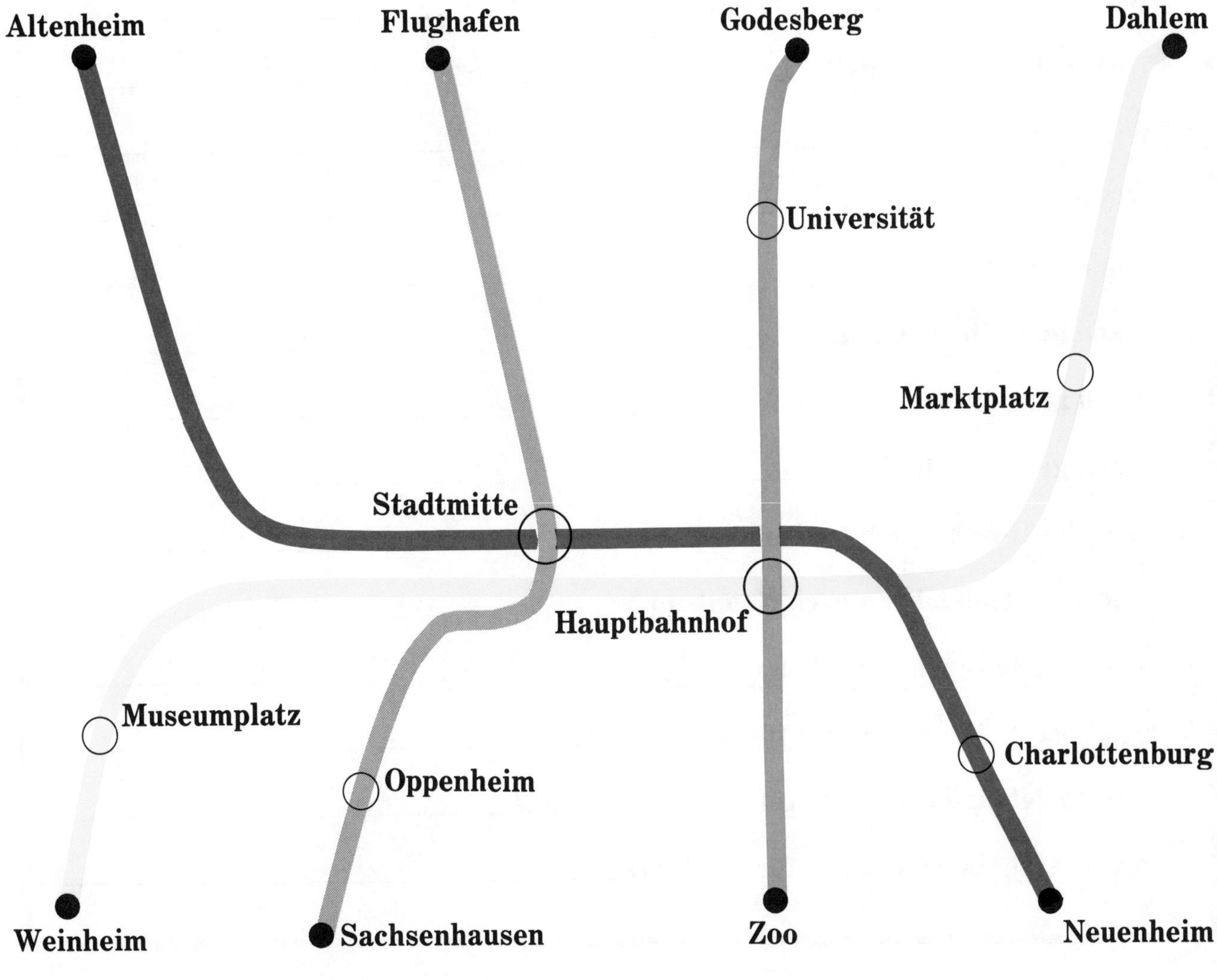

The same basic set of **Wörter und Fragen** will see you through traveling **mit dem Bus, mit der U-Bahn, mit der Straßenbahn, oder** even **mit dem Zug.**

Naturally, **die** (air-stah) **erste** (first) **Frage ist ,,wo":**

(oo-bahn-hahl-tah-shtel-ah)
Wo ist die U-Bahnhaltestelle?

(shtrah-sen-bahn-hahl-tah-shtel-ah)
Wo ist die Straßenbahnhaltestelle?

(boos-hahl-tah-shtel-ah)
Wo ist die Bushaltestelle?

Practice the following basic **Fragen** out loud **und dann** write them in the blanks (rex) **rechts.**

1. **Wo ist die U-Bahnhaltestelle?** ______________________

   Wo ist die Straßenbahnhaltestelle? ______________________

   Wo ist die Bushaltestelle? Wo ist die Bushaltestelle?

2. (vee) **Wie oft geht die U-Bahn?** ______________________

   Wie oft geht die Straßenbahn? ______________________

   Wie oft geht der Bus? ______________________

3. (vahn) **Wann geht die U-Bahn?** ______________________

   Wann geht die Straßenbahn? ______________________

   Wann geht der Bus? ______________________

4. (gate) **Geht die U-Bahn nach** (noy-en-hime) **Neuenheim?** ______________________

   Geht die Straßenbahn nach Neunheim? ______________________

   Geht der Bus nach Neuenheim? Geht der Bus nach Neuenheim?

5. (vahs) **Was kostet eine Fahrkarte** (ticket) **für die U-Bahn?** ______________________

   Was kostet eine Fahrkarte für die Straßenbahn? ______________________

   Was kostet eine Fahrkarte für den Bus? ______________________

Nun that **Sie haben** got into the swing of things, practice the following patterns aloud, substituting ,,**Straßenbahn**" for ,,**U-Bahn,**" **und** so on.

1. Wo kaufe ich eine Fahrkarte für <u>die U-Bahn</u>? für <u>die Straßenbahn</u>? für <u>den Bus</u>?

2. Wann geht die U-Bahn nach Sachsenhausen *(zahk-zen-how-zen)*? nach Altenheim *(ahl-ten-hime)*? nach Oppenheim *(oh-pen-hime)*?
zur Stadtmitte *(shtaht-mit-tah)* [city middle]? zum Zentrum *(tsen-troom)* [center]? zur Universität *(oo-ni-vair-zi-tate)* [university]? nach Dahlem? nach Godesberg *(goh-des-bairg)*?

3. Wo ist die Haltestelle für die U-Bahn nach Sachsenhausen?

Wo ist die Haltestelle für die Straßenbahn nach Altenheim?

Wo ist die Haltestelle für den Bus nach Oppenheim?

Wo ist die Haltestelle für die U-Bahn zur *(tsoor)* [to the] Stadtmitte?

Wo ist die Haltestelle für die Straßenbahn zum *(tsoom)* [to the] Zentrum?

Wo ist die Haltestelle für den Bus nach Dahlem?

Wo ist die Haltestelle für die U-Bahn nach Godesberg?

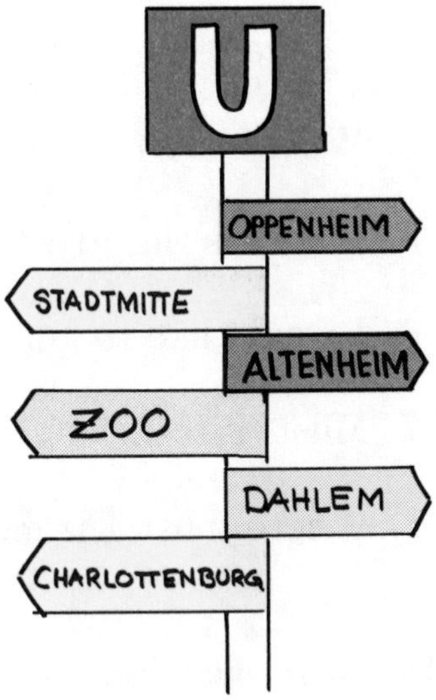

Lesen *(lay-zen)* [read] **Sie** the following **typische** *(two-pish-ah)* **Konversation und dann schreiben** *(shry-ben)* **Sie die Konversation** in the blanks **rechts.**

Welche *(vel-chah)* [which] **Linie** *(lee-nee-ah)* **geht nach Charlottenburg?** ____________________

Die rote Linie geht nach Charlottenburg. ____________________

Wie oft geht die rote Linie? ____________________

Alle *(ahl-ah)* [every] **zehn Minuten.** Alle zehn Minuten.

Muß ich umsteigen? ____________________

Ja, in der Stadtmitte. Sie steigen an [at] **der Haltestelle ,,Stadtmitte" um.**

____

Wie lange dauert es von *(fohn)* [from] **hier nach Charlottenburg?** ____________________

Es dauert 20 Minuten. ____________________

Was kostet eine Fahrkarte nach Charlottenburg? ____________________

Eine Mark neunzig. Eine Mark neunzig.

Können Sie the following thoughts into **Deutsch** translate? **Die** *(ahnt-vor-ten)* **Antworten** (answers) **sind unten.**

1. Where is the subway stop? ______________________________
2. What costs a ticket to Neuenheim? ______________________________
3. How often goes the yellow line to Weinheim? ______________________________
4. Where buy I a ticket to the city center? ______________________________
5. Where is the streetcar stop? ______________________________
6. I would like to get out. Ich möchte aussteigen.
7. Must I transfer? ______________________________
8. Where must I transfer? ______________________________

Hier sind drei Verben mehr.

(vah-shen) **waschen** = to wash

(fair-lear-en) **verlieren** = to lose

(dow-airn) **dauern** = to last

waschen ______________ ______________

Sie know the basic "plug-in" formula, so translate the following thoughts **mit** these **neuen Verben. Die** *(ahnt-vor-ten)* **Antworten sind auch unten.**

1. I wash the jacket. Ich wasche die Jacke.
2. You lose the book. ______________________________
3. It takes (lasts) 20 minutes to Charlottenburg. ______________________________
4. It takes three hours with a car. ______________________________

ANTWORTEN

1. **Wo ist die U-Bahnhaltestelle?**
2. **Was kostet (wieviel kostet) eine Karte nach Neuenheim?**
3. **Wie oft geht die gelbe Linie nach Weinheim?**
4. **Wo kaufe ich eine Karte zur Stadtmitte (zum Zentrum)?**
5. **Wo ist die Straßenbahnhaltestelle?**
6. **Ich möchte aussteigen.**
7. **Muß ich umsteigen?**
8. **Wo muß ich umsteigen?**

---

1. **Ich wasche die Jacke.**
2. **Sie verlieren das Buch.**
3. **Es dauert zwanzig Minuten nach Charlottenburg.**
4. **Es dauert drei Stunden mit dem Auto.**

(fair-kow-fen) *(kow-fen)*

Verkaufen und Kaufen

selling buying

Shopping abroad **ist** exciting. The simple everyday task of buying **einen** *(lee-tair)* **Liter Milch oder einen** *(ahp-fel)* **Apfel** (apple) becomes a challenge that **Sie** should **nun** be able to meet quickly **und** easily. Of course, **Sie** will purchase *(on-denk-en)* **Andenken** (souvenirs)**, Briefmarken, und Postkarten,** but do not forget those many other **Dinge** ranging from shoelaces to aspirin that **Sie** might need unexpectedly. *(viss-en)* **Wissen Sie** (know) the difference between **einer** *(boohk-hahnt-loong)* **Buchhandlung** (bookstore) **und einer** *(ah-poh-tay-kah)* **Apotheke?** (pharmacy) **Nein.** Let's learn about the different *(ge-shef-tah)* **Geschäfte** (shops) **und** *(lay-den)* **Läden** (stores) **in Deutschland. Unten ist ein** *(shtaht-plahn)* **Stadtplan** (map) **für eine** *(two-pish-ah)* **typische deutsche Stadt** (city)**.**

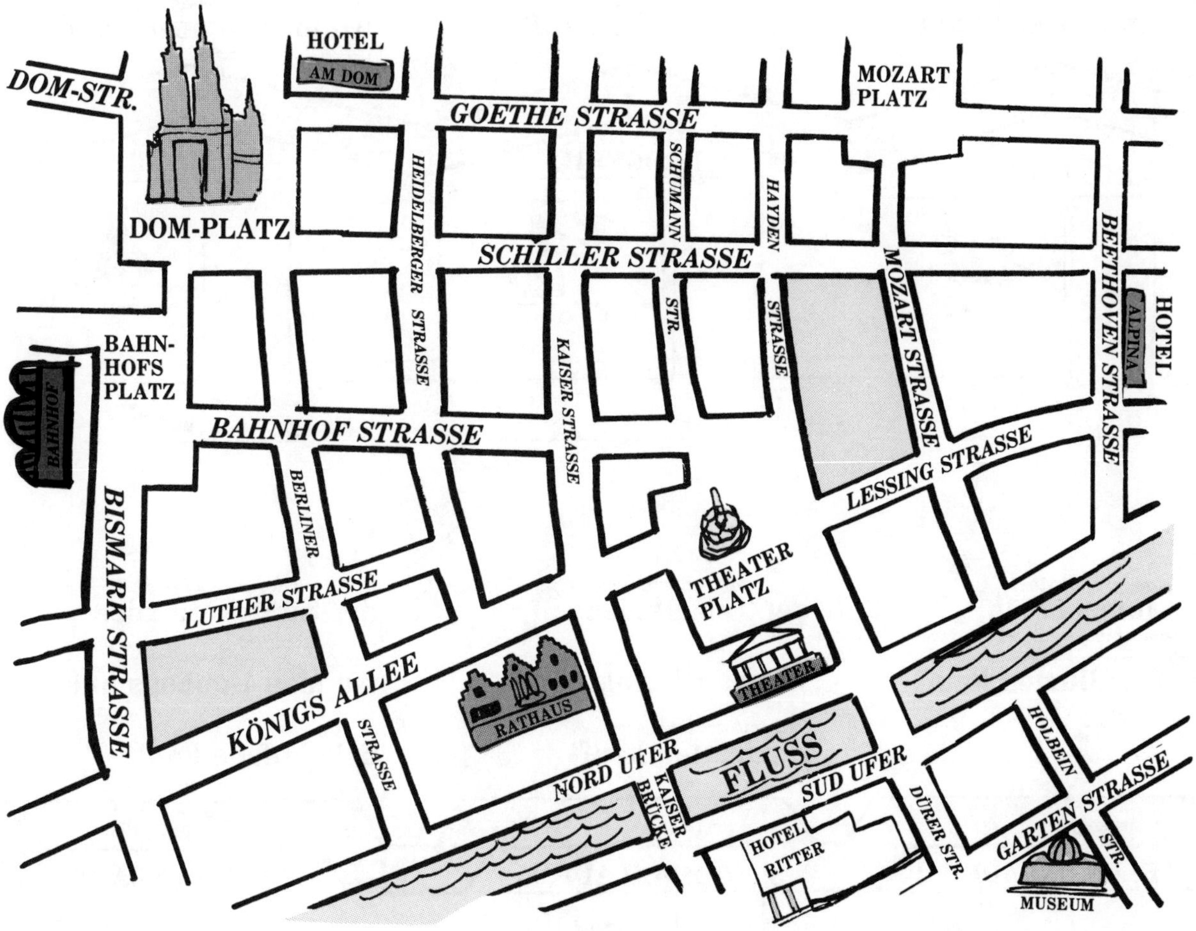

Auf den *(nex-sten)* **nächsten Seiten** (pages) **sind die Geschäfte** (shops) **in** *(dee-zair)* **dieser** (this) **Stadt.** Be sure to fill in the blanks **unter den Bildern mit den Namen** of the *(ge-shef-tah)* **Geschäfte.**

(beck-air-eye)
die Bäckerei,

(mahn) *(kowft)*
wo man Brot kauft
one buys

(mets-gair-eye)
die Metzgerei,

(flysh)
wo man Fleisch kauft
one meat

(vesh-air-eye)
die Wäscherei,

(kly-dair) *(vesht)*
wo man Kleider wäscht
clothes washes

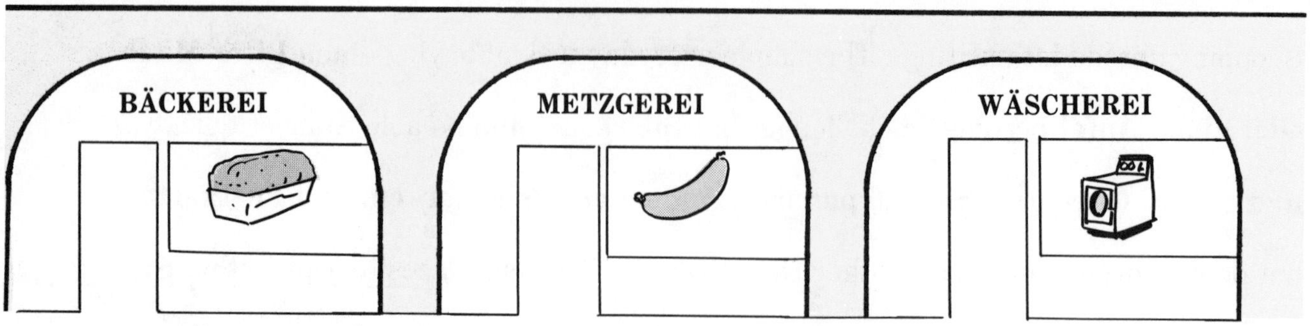

die Bäckerei

(kohn-dee-tor-eye)
die Konditorei,
café

wo man Kaffee trinkt

(droh-gih-ree)
die Drogerie,
drugstore

(zigh-fah)
wo man Seife kauft

(ah-poh-tay-kah)
die Apotheke,
pharmacy

(ahs-peer-een)
wo man Aspirin kauft
aspirin

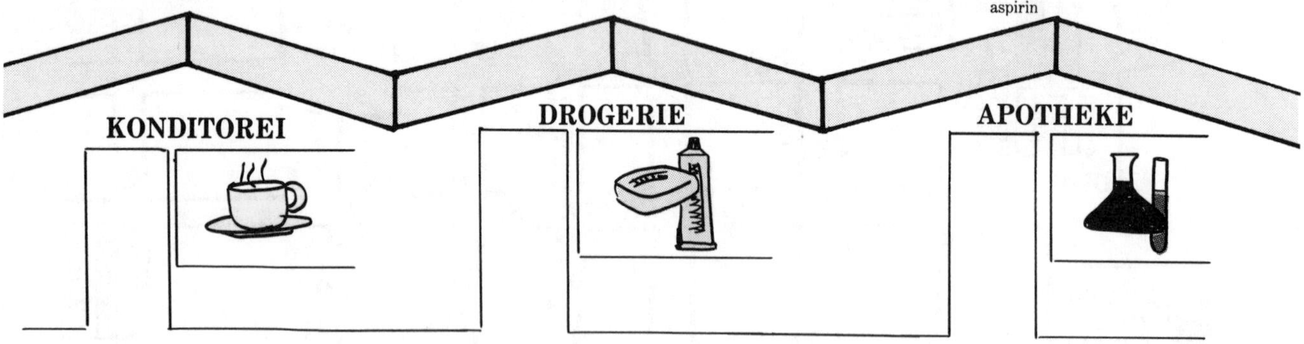

die Apotheke

(bloo-men-lah-den)
der Blumenladen,
flower shop

wo man Blumen kauft

(tah-bahk-lah-den)
der Tabakladen,

wo man Tabak und

(tsih-gah-ret-ten)
Zigaretten kauft

(zews-vah-ren-lah-den)
der Süßwarenladen,
candy store

(bohn-bohns)
wo man Bonbons und

Schokolade kauft

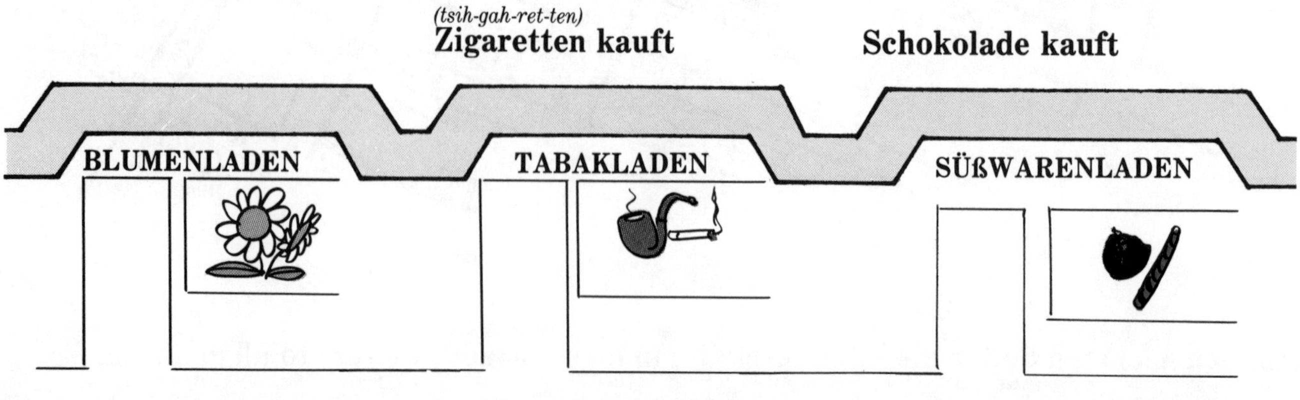

das Milchgeschäft, *(milsh-ge-sheft)* dairy
wo man Milch kauft *(mahn)*

das Fotogeschäft, *(foh-toh-ge-sheft)* camera store
wo man Film kauft

das Gemüsegeschäft, *(ge-mew-zah-ge-sheft)* vegetable store
wo man Gemüse kauft

_______________ _______________ _______________

der Parkplatz, *(park-plahts)* parking lot
wo man Autos parkt *(mahn)*

der Friseur, *(frih-zur)* hairdresser
wo man Haar schneidet *(shny-det)* cuts

der Schneider, *(shny-dair)* tailor
wo man Kleider macht *(kly-dair)* clothes, makes

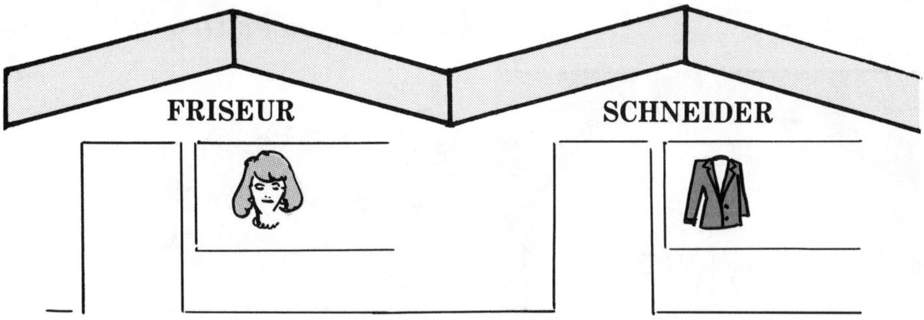

_______________ _______________ der Schneider

das Postamt, *(post-ahmt)* post office
wo man Briefmarken kauft

das Polizeiamt, *(poh-lih-tsigh-ahmt)* police station
wo man die Polizei findet

die Bank, *(bahnk)*
wo man Geld wechselt und *(vex-selt)* exchanges
man einen Scheck einlöst *(sheck)* check, *(ine-lurst)* cashes

_______________ _______________ _______________

(lay-bens-mih-tel-ge-sheft)
das Lebensmittelgeschäft,
grocery store
wo man Fleisch, Obst und Milch kauft

(fine-kohst-ge-sheft)
das Feinkostgeschäft,
delicatessen
wo man Spezialitäten kauft

(ohpst-ge-sheft)
das Obstgeschäft,
fruit shop
wo man Obst kauft

_______________ _______________ _______________

(key-noh)
das Kino,
movie theater
wo man Filme sieht *(zeet)*
sees

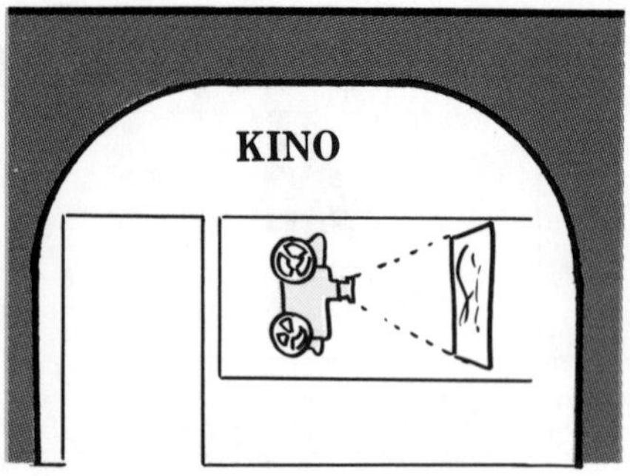

das Kino

(key-ohsk)
der Kiosk,
newsstand
wo man Zeitungen und Zeitschriften kauft

____

(rye-nih-goong)
die Reinigung,
dry cleaners
wo man Kleider chemisch reinigt
chemically, cleans

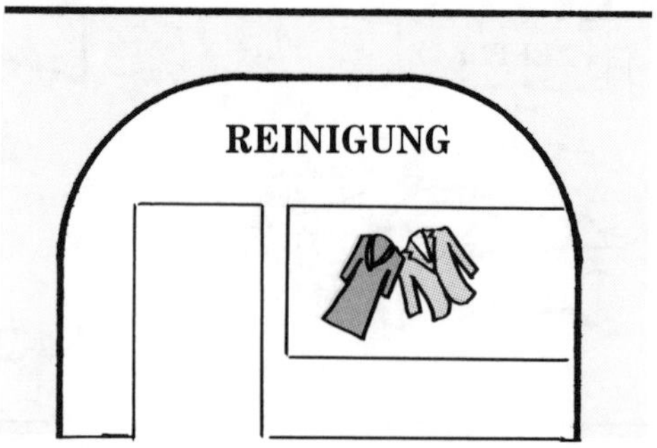

____

(shripe-vah-ren-hahnt-loong)
die Schreibwarenhandlung,
stationery store
wo man Papier, Bleistifte, und Kulis kauft

(boohk-hahnt-loong)
die Buchhandlung,
bookstore
wo man Bücher kauft und verkauft

(vah-ren-house)
das Warenhaus,
department store
wo man alles kaufen kann
(see Step 22)

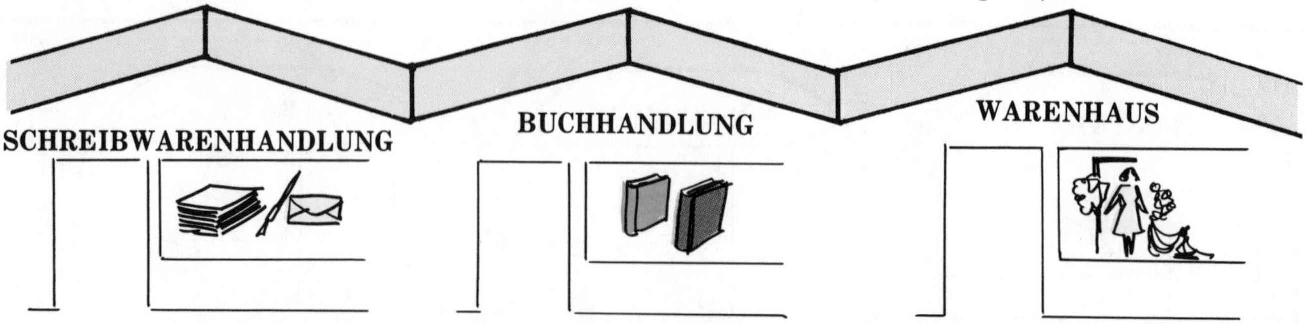

_______________ _______________ _______________

(markt)
der Markt, wo man
market

Gemüse und Obst kauft

____

(on-denk-en-lah-den)
der Andenkenladen,
souvenir store

wo man Andenken kauft

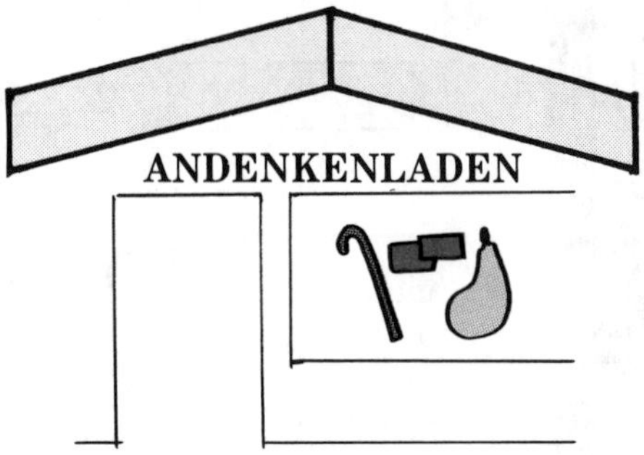

____

(tahnk-shtel-ah)
die Tankstelle,
gas station

wo man Benzin kauft

die Tankstelle

(ry-zah-bew-roh)
das Reisebüro,
travel office

wo man Flugkarten kauft

(uhr-mah-kair)
der Uhrmacher,
watchmaker

wo man Uhren kauft

(fish-hahnt-loong)
die Fischhandlung,
fish store

wo man Fisch kauft

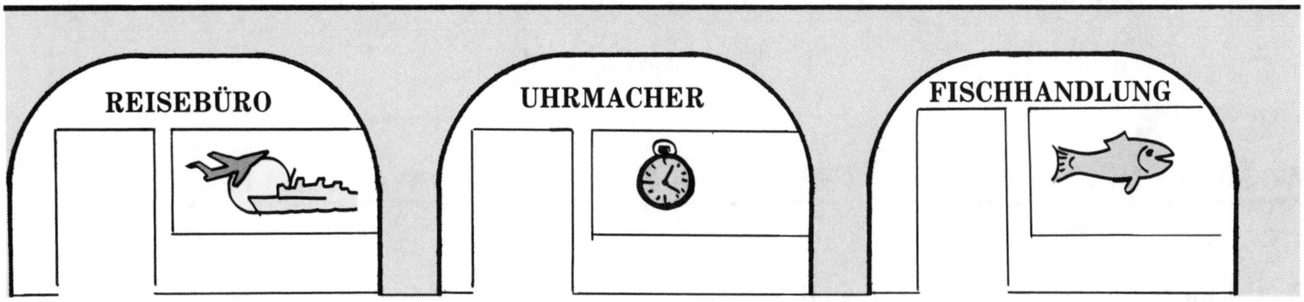

_______________ _______________ _______________

(vahn) **Wann sind die deutschen Geschäfte auf** (open)? Normally, **die deutschen Geschäfte sind Montag bis** (until) **Freitag,** *(fohn)* **von 8:00 oder 9:00 Uhr bis 18 Uhr 30 auf. Viele** (many) **Geschäfte** will close over the lunch hour **(12:00 bis 14:00),** so plan accordingly. **Am Samstag sind die Geschäfte von 8:00 oder 9:00 Uhr nur bis 14:00 Uhr auf. Am Sonntag sind die Geschäfte** *(tsoo)* **zu!** (closed) On the first **Samstag** of every **Monat,** there is what is known as *(long-air)* **„langer** (long) **Samstag."** On this **Samstag, die Geschäfte** *(bly-ben)* **bleiben** (remain) **bis 18:00 Uhr auf. Gibt es** (is there) anything else which makes **deutsche Geschäfte** different from **amerikanische Geschäfte? Ja.** Look at **das Bild auf der nächsten Seite.**

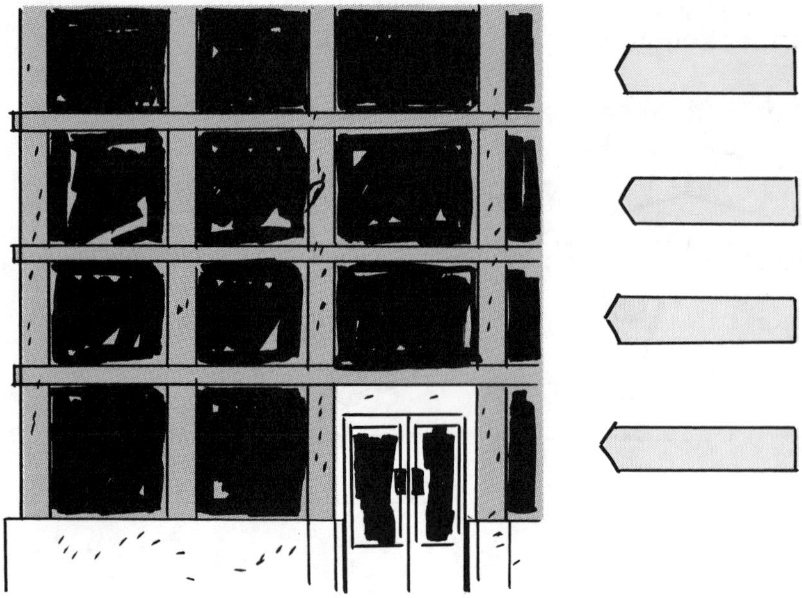

3. *(shtoke)* **Stock**

2. *(shtoke)* **Stock**

1. *(shtoke)* **Stock**

(airt-ge-shohs) **Erdgeschoß oder** *(par-tair-ah)* **Parterre**

In Deutschland, the ground floor **heißt** exactly that — **das** *(airt-ge-shohs)* **Erdgeschoß** (earth floor)**.** The first floor **ist** the next floor up **und** so on. Now that **Sie** know **die Namen für die deutschen Geschäfte,** let's practice shopping.

I. First step — **Wo!**

Wo ist das Milchgeschäft? **Wo ist die Bank?** **Wo ist das Kino?**

Go through **die Geschäfte** introduced in this Step **und** ask **„wo"** **mit** each **Geschäft.** Another way of asking **wo** is to ask

Gibt es (is there) **ein Milchgeschäft in der** (the) *(nay-ah)* **Nähe** (vicinity)**?** **Gibt es eine Bank in der Nähe?**

Go through **die Geschäfte** again using this new question.

II. Next step — tell them **was Sie** are looking for, **brauchen oder möchten!**

1) **Ich brauche . . .** Ich brauche ______________________________

2) **Haben Sie . . . ?** ______________________________

3) **Ich möchte . . .** ______________________________

Ich brauche einen Bleistift.

Haben Sie einen Bleistift?

Ich möchte einen Bleistift.

Ich brauche einen Liter Buttermilch.

Haben Sie einen Liter Buttermilch?

Ich möchte einen Liter Buttermilch.

Go through the glossary at the end of this **Buch und** select **zwanzig** *(tsvahn-tsig)* (twenty) **Wörter.** Drill the above patterns **mit diesen zwanzig Wörtern.** Don't cheat. Drill them **heute. Nun,** take **zwanzig Wörter mehr von Ihrem** *(ear-em)* (your) **Wörterbuch** *(vur-tair-boohk)* (dictionary) **und** do the same.

III. Next step — find out **wieviel es kostet.**

1) **Was** *(vahs)* **kostet das?** ______________________________

2) **Wieviel** *(vee-feel)* **kostet das?** ______________________________

Was kostet der Bleistift?

Wieviel kostet der Bleistift?

Was kostet der Liter Buttermilch?

Wieviel kostet der Liter Buttermilch?

Using the same **Wörter** that **Sie** selected **oben,** drill **diese Fragen auch.**

IV. If **Sie wissen nicht, wo** to find something, **Sie fragen**

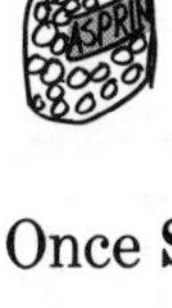

Wo kann ich Aspirin *(ahs-peer-een)* (aspirin) **kaufen?**

Wo kann ich eine Sonnenbrille *(zoh-nen-bril-ah)* (sunglasses) **kaufen?**

Once **Sie finden was Sie** would like, **Sie sagen, Ich möchte das, bitte.**

Oder, if **Sie** would not like **es, Ich möchte das nicht.**

Sie sind nun all set to shop for anything!

Step 22

das Warenhaus *(vah-ren-house)* department store

At this point, **Sie** should just about be ready for your **Reise** *(ry-zah)* **nach Deutschland. Sie** have gone shopping for those last-minute odds 'n ends. Most likely, the store directory at your local **Warenhaus** *(vah-ren-house)* did **nicht** look like the one **unten! Viele Wörter wissen** (know) **Sie** already **und Sie** could guess at **viele** others. **Sie wissen** that **„Kinder" ist das deutsche Wort für** "children," so if **Sie brauchen** something **für das Kind, Sie** would probably look on **Stock** *(shtoke)* **zwei oder drei** *(dry)*, **nicht wahr?**

6. STOCK	Brot-Backwaren Cafeteria Delikatessen Spirituosen	Geflügel Lebensmittel Obst Gemüse	Tiefkühlkost Weine Wild Fleisch
5. STOCK	Betten Bettfedern Plastik	Kleinmöbel Lampen Orient	Teppiche Bilder
4. STOCK	Bestecke Elektro-Artikel Glas	Haushaltwaren Hobby Küchenmöbel	Schlüsselbar Keramik Porzellan
3. STOCK	Bücher Fernsehen Kindermöbel Kinderwagen	Spielwaren Musikinstrumente Rundfunk Schreibwaren Schallplatten	Tabakwaren Teeraum Zeitschriften Zeitungen
2. STOCK	Alles für das Kind Damenbekleidung	Herrenbekleidung Damenhüte	Fundbüro Kundendienst
1. STOCK	Autozubehör Damenwäsche Taschentücher	Badeartikel Schuhe Handarbeiten	Bettwäsche Sportartikel
E	Foto-Optik Herrenhüte Schirme Schmuck	Handschuhe Lederwaren Strümpfe Uhren	Herrenartikel Parfümerie Süßwaren

Let's start a check list **für Ihre Reise.** Besides **Kleider** *(kly-dair)* (clothing), **was brauchen Sie?**

Was nehmen *(nay-men)* (take) **Sie nach Europa?**

(pah-ss) **der Paß** ______________ ☐

(flook-kar-tah) **die Flugkarte** ______________ ☐

(koh-fair) **der Koffer** der Koffer ☑

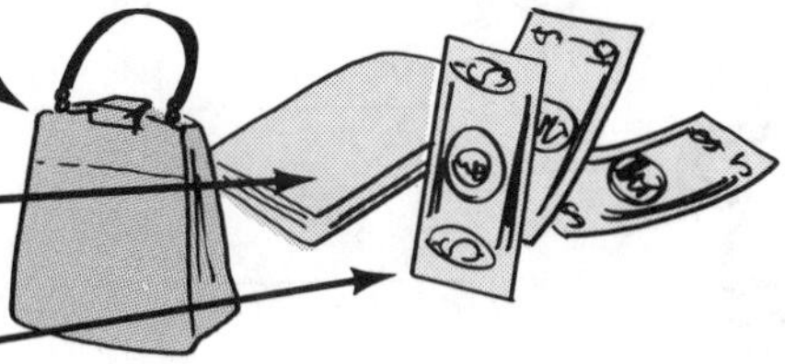

(hahnt-tah-shah) **die Handtasche** ______________ ☐

(breef-tah-shah) **die Brieftasche** ______________ ☐

(gelt) **das Geld** ______________ ☐

(kah-mair-ah) **die Kamera** ______________ ☐

der Film ______________ ☐

(nay-men) **Nehmen** (take) **Sie die nächsten acht** labels **und** label *(dee-zah)* **diese** (these) **Dinge heute.** Better yet, assemble them **in einer Ecke** (corner) of your **Haus.**

Reisen Sie nach Deutschland im Sommer oder im Winter? Vergessen (forget) **Sie nicht . . .**

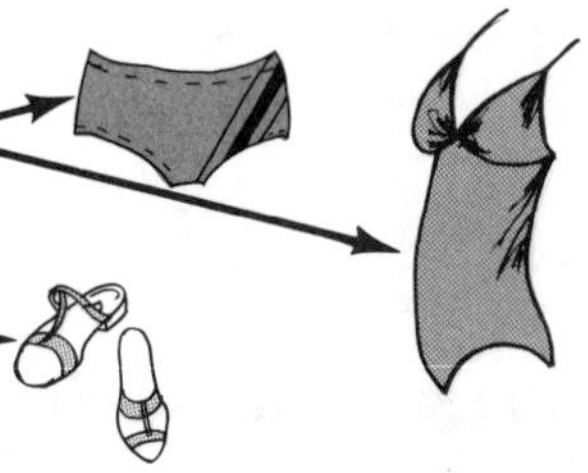

(bah-da-on-tsook) **der Badeanzug** ______________ ☐

(zahn-dah-len) **die Sandalen** ______________ ☐

Vergessen Sie auch nicht the basic toiletries!

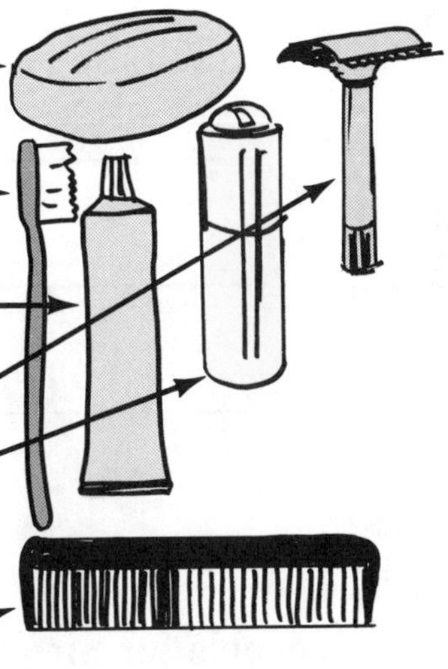

(zigh-fah) **die Seife** die Seife ☑

(tsahn-bewr-stah) **die Zahnbürste** ______________ ☐

(tsahn-pah-stah) **die Zahnpaste** ______________ ☐

(rah-zeer-mes-sair) **das Rasiermesser** ______________ ☐

(day-oh) **das Deo** ______________ ☐

(kahm) **der Kamm** ______________ ☐

For the rest of the **Dinge,** let's start **mit** the outside layers **und** work our way in.

(mahn-tel)
der Mantel — der Mantel ☑

(ray-gen-mahn-tel)
der Regenmantel ☐

(ray-gen-shirm)
der Regenschirm ☐

(hahnt-shoo-ah)
die Handschuhe ☐

(hoot)
der Hut ☐

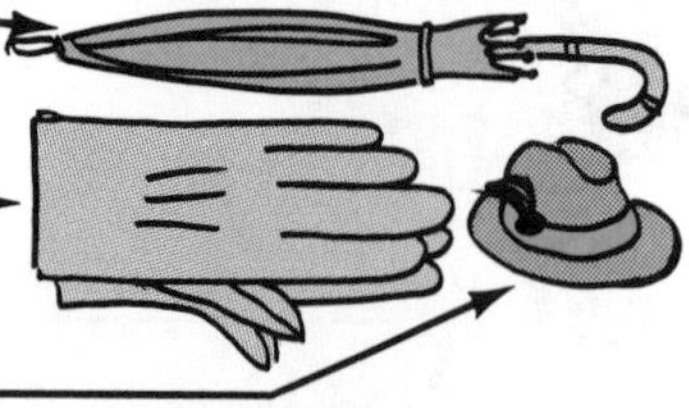

(shtee-fel)
die Stiefel ☐

(shoo-ah)
die Schuhe ☐

(zoh-ken)
die Socken — die Socken ☑

(shtroompf-hoh-zah)
die Strumpfhose ☐

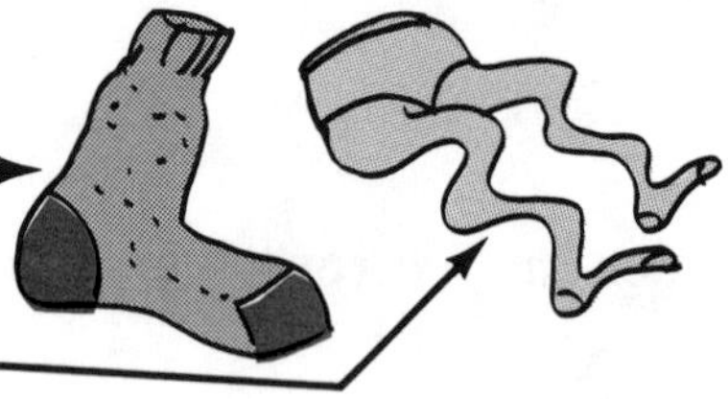

Nehmen *(nay-men)* (take) **Sie die nächsten fünfzehn** labels **und** label **diese Dinge.** Check **und** make sure that **sie sind sauber** *(zow-bair)* (clean) **und** ready for your trip. Be sure to do the same **mit** the rest of the **Dinge Sie packen** *(pah-ken)* (pack)**.** Check them off on this **Liste** as **Sie** organize them. From **nun** on, **Sie haben „Zahnpaste"** **und nicht** "toothpaste."

(shlahf-on-tsook)
der Schlafanzug ☐

(nahkt-hemt)
das Nachthemd ☐

(bah-da-mahn-tel)
der Bademantel ☐

(house-shoo-ah)
die Hausschuhe ☐

Der Bademantel und die Hausschuhe können auch double **für Sie** at the **Schwimmbad** *(shvim-baht)* (swimming pool)**!**

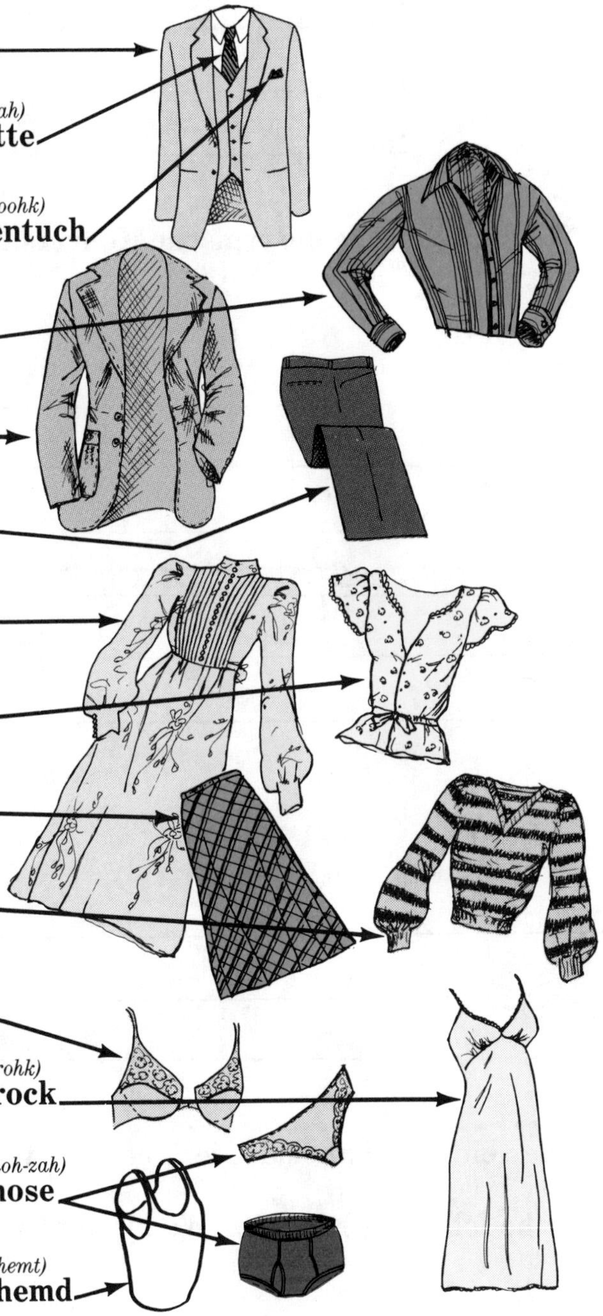

(on-tsook) **der Anzug** ______________________ ☐

(krah-vah-tah) **die Krawatte** ______________________ ☐

(tah-shen-toohk) **das Taschentuch** ______________________ ☐

(hemt) **das Hemd** ______________________ ☐

(yah-kah) **die Jacke** ______________________ ☐

(hoh-zah) **die Hose** ____die Hose____ ☑

(klite) **das Kleid** ______________________ ☐

(bloo-zah) **die Bluse** ______________________ ☐

(rohk) **der Rock** ______________________ ☐

(pool-ee) **der Pulli** ______________________ ☐

(bay-hah) **der BH** ______________________ ☐

(oon-tair-rohk) **der Unterrock** ______________________ ☐

(oon-tair-hoh-zah) **die Unterhose** ______________________ ☐

(oon-tair-hemt) **das Unterhemd** ______________________ ☐

Having assembled **diese Dinge, Sie sind** ready **für Ihre Reise.** However, being human means occasionally forgetting something. Look again at the **Warenhaus** directory.

Im welchem (which) **Stock** *(shtoke)* **finden Sie . . .**

Kleider für einen Mann?	**Im** ______________ **Stock.**
einen Hut für eine Dame (Frau)?	**Im** ______________ **Stock.**
Bücher?	**Im** _____3_____ **Stock.**
(dah-men-vesh-ah) **Damenwäsche?** (ladies' underclothing)	**Im** ______________ **Stock.**

Schuhe? **Im** ____________ **Stock.**

Socken (Strümpfe)? **Im** ____________ **Stock.**

Kleider für die Dame? **Im** ____________ **Stock.**

Nun, just remember your basic **Fragen. Wiederholen Sie die typische Konversation unten** out loud **und dann** by filling in the blanks.

Wo finde ich eine Damenhose? ____________

In der Damenabteilung. (women's department) ____________

Wo ist die Damenabteilung? ____________

Im zweiten Stock. Im zweiten Stock.

Wo finde ich Seife und Zahnpaste? ____________

Im Erdgeschoß. ____________

Vergessen Sie auch nicht zu *(tsoo)* (to) **fragen . . .**

Wo ist der Fahrstuhl? (elevator) ____________

Wo ist die Treppe? (steps) ____________

Wo ist die Rolltreppe? (escalator) ____________

Whether **Sie brauchen eine Damenhose oder ein Herrenhemd, die** necessary **Wörter sind** the same! Practice your **neue Wörter mit** the following **Kleider** *(kly-dair)* (clothing). **Wo ist die Bluse?**

Wo ist...

Clothing Sizes: **FRAUEN**

(vel-chah) *(grur-sah)*
Welche Größe?
which size

____

Es paßt.
It fits

____

Es paßt nicht.
It fits not

Es paßt nicht.

Schuhe

American	5	5½	6	6½	7	7½	8	8½	9
Continental	35	35	36	37	38	38	38	39	40

Kleider

American	8	10	12	14	16	18
Continental	36	38	40	42	44	46

Blusen, Pullis

American	32	34	36	38	40	42	44
Continental	40	42	44	46	48	50	52

Clothing Sizes: **HERREN**

(nay-mah)
Ich nehme dieses.
take this

____

Was kostet das?

____

Das ist alles. Danke.
all

____

Schuhe

American	7	7½	8	8½	9	9½	10	10½	11	11½
Continental	39	40	41	42	43	43	44	44	45	45

Kleider

American	34	36	38	40	42	44	46	48
Continental	44	46	48	50	52	54	56	58

Hemden

American	14	14½	15	15½	16	16½	17	17½
Continental	36	37	38	39	40	41	42	43

Nun, Sie sind ready **für Ihre Reise. Sie wissen alles, was Sie brauchen.** The next Step will give you a quick review of international road signs **und** then **Sie** are off to the **Flughafen.**

Gute Reise! Viel Spaß!

Step 23

= **Dangerous Intersection**

Hier sind some of the most important **deutsche** **Straßenschildern** *(shtrah-sen-shill-dair)* (street signs). **Fahren Sie** **vorsichtig** *(for-zeehk-teeg)* (carefully)! **Gute Reise!**

Danger

Dangerous curve

Dangerous intersection

Closed to all vehicles

Prohibited for motor vehicles

Prohibited for motor vehicles on Sundays and holidays

No entry

Stop

Main road ahead, yield the right of way

You have the right of way

Additional sign indicating the right of way

One-way street

Dead-end street

Detour

Traffic circle

No left turn

No U-turn

No parking

No parking or waiting

No passing

Speed limit

End of speed limit

Beginning of **Autobahn**

Railroad crossing
240 meters

Railroad crossing
160 meters

Railroad crossing
80 meters

Customs

Federal Highway
Number

City limit
(50 km/h speed
limit)

Parking permitted

Road ends, water
ahead

GLOSSARY

A

ab .... away from, leaves
Abend, der .... evening
Abendessen, das .... dinner
abends .... evenings
abfahren .... to depart
Abfahrt, die .... departure
abnehmen .... to remove
Abteil, das .... compartment
Abteilung, die .... department
abwarten .... to wait for
acht .... eight
achtzehn .... eighteen
achtzig .... eighty
Adresse, die .... address
alle .... all, everyone
alles .... everything
Alphabet, das .... alphabet
alt .... old
am (= an dem) .... at the, on the
Amerika, das .... America
Amerikaner, der .... American
amerikanisch .... American
Amtsdeutsch, das . . bureaucratic German
an .... on, at, arrives
Andenken, das (die Andenken) . souvenir
Andenkenladen, der ...... souvenir shop
ankommen .... to arrive
Ankunft, die .... arrival
Anruf, der .... call, telephone call
anrufen .... to call up
Antwort, die (die Antworten) ... answer
Anzug, der .... suit
Apfel, der .... apple
Apotheke, die .... pharmacy
Appetit, der .... appetite
April, der .... April
arbeiten .... to work
arm .... poor
Arzt, der .... physician
auch .... also
auf .... on top of, open
auf Deutsch .... in German
auf Englisch .... in English
Auf Wiederhören! . . Hear from you again!
Auf Wiedersehen! .... See you again!
Aufschnittplatte, die ..... cold cut plate
Augenblick, der .... moment
August, der .... August
aus .... out of, from
Ausfahrt, die .... exit (for vehicles)
Ausgang, der .... exit (for people)
Auskunft, die .... information
ausland .... abroad
Ausland, das .... foreign country
Auslandsgespräche, die . phone calls to a foreign country
aussteigen .... to get out
Auto, das (die Autos) .... car
Autobahn, die .... freeway
Autoreise, die .... car trip

B

BH, der .... brassiere
Bäckerei, die .... bakery
Backteig, der .... batter
Badeanzug, der .... bathing suit
Bademantel, der .... bathrobe
baden .... to bathe
Badetuch, das .... bath towel
Badezimmer, das .... bathroom
Bahnhof, der .... train station
Bahnsteig, der .... railway platform
Ball, der .... ball
Ballettkarte, die .... ballet ticket
Banane, die .... banana
Bank, die .... bank
Beefsteak, das .... beefsteak
beendetem .... concluded
beginnen .... to begin
bei .... by, near
Beilagen, die .... supplements
belegt .... toppings
Bemerkungen, die ...... remarks, notes
Benzin, das .... gasoline
Berg, der (die Berge) .... mountain
besetzt .... occupied
besser .... better
bestellen .... to order
Bett, das .... bed
Bettdecke, die ...... blanket, bedspread
bezahlen .... to pay
Bier, das (die Biere) .... beer
Bierhalle, die .... beerhall
Bild, das (die Bilder) .... picture
billig .... cheap
bin .... am
bis .... until
bitte .... please
blau, blaue .... blue
bleiben .... to remain, stay
Bleistift, der .... pencil
Blume, die (die Blumen) .... flower
Blumenladen, der .... flower shop
Bluse, die (die Blusen) .... blouse
Bonbons, die .... candy
Boot, das .... boat
brauchen .... to need
braun .... brown
Brief, der (die Briefe) .... letter
Briefkasten, der .... mailbox
Briefmarke, die .... stamp
Brieftasche, die ..... wallet, pocketbook
Brille, die .... eyeglasses
bringen .... to bring
Brot, das .... bread
Brötchen, das .... roll
Bruder, der .... brother
Buch, das (die Bücher) .... book
buchen .... to book, reserve
Buchhandlung, die .... bookstore
bunt .... multi-colored
Büro, das .... office, study
Bus, der (die Busse) .... bus
Bushaltestelle, die .... bus stop
Butter, die .... butter
Buttermilch, die .... buttermilk

C

Café, das .... café
Celsius .... centigrade

D

DM .... abbre. for German mark
D-Zug, der .... express train
Dame, die (die Damen) .... lady
Damenabteilung, die .... women's department
Damenhose, die .... ladies' pants
Damenwäsche, die .... women's underclothing
danke .... thank you
Danke schön! ..... Thank you very much!
dann .... then
das .... the, that
dauert/dauern .... lasts/to take time
dazu .... besides
Decke, die .... ceiling, cover
dem .... the
den .... the
Deo, das .... deodorant
der .... the, of the
des .... the, of the
Deutsch, das .... German
deutsch, deutschen .... German
Deutsche Mark, die ...... German mark
Deutschland, das .... Germany
Dezember, der .... December
dick .... thick
die .... the
Dienstag, der .... Tuesday
dieser, diesen .... this, that, these
Ding, das (die Dinge) .... thing
Doktor, der .... doctor
Dollar, der .... dollar
Donnerstag, der .... Thursday
dort .... there
drei .... three
dreißig .... thirty
dreizehn .... thirteen
Drogerie, die .... drugstore
dünn .... thin
durch .... through
durstig .... thirsty
Dusche, die .... shower

E

E-Zug, der .... medium-fast train
Ecke, die .... corner
Ei, das (die Eier) .... egg
Eierspeisen, die .... egg dishes
Eilzüge, die .... medium-fast trains
ein .... a
ein bißchen .... a little
ein paar .... a pair, a couple
eine .... a
einem .... a
einen .... a
einer .... a, of a
eines .... a, of a
einfach .... one-way, simple
Einfahrt, die ..... entrance (for vehicles)
Eingang, der ...... entrance (for people)
einhängen .... to hang up
einlöst/einlösen .... redeems/to redeem
Einpfennigstück, das . . one-pfennig piece
eins .... one
einsteigen .... to get in, board
einstempeln .... to cancel, punch
einwerfen .... to throw in
Eis, das .... ice cream
Eisbecher mit Früchten, der . . ice-cream cup with fruit
Elefant, der .... elephant
elf .... eleven
Eltern, die .... parents
Entschuldigung .... excuse me
er .... he
Erdgeschoß, das .... ground floor
erste Klasse .... first class
es .... it
es gibt .... there is, there are
es tut mir leid .... I am sorry
essen .... to eat
Essen, das .... meal
Eßzimmer, das .... dining room
Etage, die .... floor, story
Europa, das .... Europe
europäisch .... European
evangelisch .... Protestant

F

fahren .... to go, drive, travel
Fahrenheit, die .... Fahrenheit
Fahrkarte, die .... ticket
Fahrplan, der .... timetable
Fahrrad, das .... bicycle
Fahrstuhl, der .... elevator
Fahrt, die .... ride, drive, trip
Farbe, die (die Farben) .... color
Februar, der .... February
Feinkostgeschäft, das ..... delicatessen
Fenster, das .... window

Ferngespräch, das (die Ferngespräche) . . . . .long-distance telephone call
Fernseher, der . . . . television set
Fernsprecher, der . . . . telephone
Fernsprechverzeichnis, das . . . telephone book
Fernsprechzelle, die . . . . telephone booth
Fertige Gerichte, die . . . . entrees
Feuer, das . . . . fire
Film, der (die Filme) . . . . film
finden . . . . to find
Firma, die . . . . firm, company
Fisch, der . . . . fish
Fischgerichte, die . . . . fish entrees
Fischhandlung, die . . . . fish store
Flasche, die (die Flaschen) . . . . bottle
Fleisch, das . . . . meat
fliegen . . . . to fly
Flughafen, der . . . . airport
Flugkarte, die . . . . airplane ticket
Flugreise, die . . . . airplane trip
Flugzeug, das . . . . airplane
Formular, das . . . . form
Fotogeschäft, das . . . . photo shop
Frage, die (die Fragen) . . . . question
fragen . . . . to ask
Frau, die (die Frauen) . . . . . woman, Mrs.
Fräulein, das . . . . young lady, Miss
frei . . . . free of charge, available
Freitag, der . . . . Friday
Fremdenverkehrsamt, das . . . . . . tourist office
friert/friern . . . . freezes/to freeze
frisch . . . . fresh
Friseur, der . . . . hairdresser
Frühling, der . . . . spring
Frühstück, das . . . . breakfast
Frühstücksportion, die . . . . . . breakfast portion
fünf . . . . five
Fünfhundertmarkschein, der . 500-mark bill
Fünfmarkschein, der . . . . 5-mark bill
Fünfmarkstück, das . . . . 5-mark coin
Fünfpfennigstück, das . . . 5-pfennig coin
fünfzehn . . . . fifteen
fünfzig . . . . fifty
Fünfzigmarkschein, der . . . . 50-mark bill
Fünfzigpfennigstück, das . . . 50-pfennig coin
Fundbüro, das . . . . . lost-and-found office
für . . . . for

G

g'suffa . . . . drink
Gabel, die . . . . fork
Garage, die . . . . garage
Garten, der . . . . garden, yard
Gasthaus, das . . . . restaurant, inn
Gasthof, der . . . . hotel, inn
gebacken . . . . baked
gebraten . . . . roasted, fried
Geflügel, das . . . . poultry
gegrillt . . . . grilled
geht/gehen . . . . goes/to go
gekocht . . . . cooked, boiled
gekochtes Ei . . . . boiled egg
gelb . . . . yellow
Geld, das . . . . money
Geldscheine, die . . . . bank notes
Geldstücke, die . . . . coins
gemischter Salat . . . . mixed salad
gemischtes Eis . . . . mixed ice cream
Gemüse, das . . . . vegetables
Gemüsegeschäft, das . . . vegetable store
genau . . . . exactly
genau so . . . . just as
genug . . . . enough
geradeaus . . . . straight ahead
Geschäft, das (die Geschäfte) . . . . . store
Gespräch, das . . . . conversation
gestern . . . . yesterday
gesund . . . . healthy
Glas, das . . . . glass
Gleis, das . . . . track
Glück, das . . . . luck
Goethe Museum, das . . . Goethe Museum
Grad, der . . . . degree
Gras, das . . . . grass
grau . . . . gray
Grill- und Pfannengerichte, die . . . . grilled and fried entrees
groß . . . . large
Größe, die . . . . size
Großeltern, die . . . . grandparents
Großmutter, die . . . . grandmother
Großvater, der . . . . grandfather
grün . . . . green
gut, gutes, gute . . . . good

H

Haar, das . . . . hair
haben . . . . to have
halb . . . . half
hallo . . . . hello
Haltestelle, die . . . . . transportation stop
Hammel, der . . . . mutton
Hand, die . . . . hand
Handapparat, der . . . . telephone receiver
Handschuhe, die . . . . gloves
Handtasche, die . . . . purse
Handtuch, das . . . . hand towel
hat/haben . . . . has/to have
Hat's geschmeckt? . . . . Did it taste good?
Hauptausgang, der . . . . main exit
Hauptbahnhof, der . . . main train station
Haupteingang, der . . . . . . main entrance
Haus, das . . . . house
Hausschuhe, die . . . . slippers
Hbf . . . . abbre. for main train station
heiß . . . . hot
heißt/heißen . . . . . . is called/to be called
Hemd, das (die Hemden) . . . . shirt
Herbst, der . . . . fall
Herr, der (die Herren) . . . gentleman, Mr.
Herr Ober! . . . . Waiter!
Herrenhemd, das . . . . man's shirt
heute . . . . today
hier . . . . here
hin und zurück . . . . there and back
hinter . . . . behind
hoch . . . . high
Hofbräuhaus, das . . . . brewery
Hose, die . . . . trousers
Hotel, das . . . . hotel
Hotelmanager, der . . . . . . hotel manager
Hotelrechnung, die . . . . hotel bill
Hotelzimmer, das . . . . hotel room
Hund, der . . . . dog
hundert . . . . hundred
Hundertmarkschein, der . . 100-mark bill
hungrig . . . . hungry
Hut, der . . . . hat

I

ich I
Idee, die . . . . idea
Ihnen . . . . to you
Ihr, Ihre, Ihrem . . . . your
im (= in dem) . . . . in, in the
in . . . . in
Information, die . . . . information
inland . . . . inland, domestic
Inter-City Züge, die . . . . inter-city trains
ist/sein . . . . is/to be

J

ja . . . . yes
Jacke, die . . . . jacket
Jahr, das (die Jahre) . . . . year
Januar, der . . . . January
jüdisch . . . . Jewish
Juli, der . . . . July
jung . . . . young
Juni, der . . . . June

K

Kabine, die . . . . booth
Kaffee und Kuchen . . . . . coffee and cake
Kaffee, der . . . . coffee
Kakao, der . . . . cocoa
Kalb, das . . . . veal
Kalender, der . . . . calendar
kalt . . . . cold
kalte Speisen . . . . cold meals
Kamera, die . . . . camera
Kamm, der . . . . comb
kann/können . . . . can/to be able to
Kännchen, das . . . . pot
Karte, die (die Karten) . .card, ticket, map
Kartoffeln, die . . . . potatoes
Käse, der . . . . cheese
katholisch . . . . Catholic
Katze, die . . . . cat
kauft/kaufen . . . . buys/to buy
kein Ausgang . . . . no exit
kein Eingang . . . . no entrance
Keller, der . . . . cellar
Kellner, der . . . . waiter
Kellnerin, die . . . . waitress
Kilometer, der . . . . kilometer
Kind, das (die Kinder) . . . . child
Kinderteller, der . . . . children's plate
Kino, das . . . . movie theater
Kiosk, der . . . . newsstand
Kirche, die . . . . church
Kleid, das . . . . dress
Kleider, die . . . . clothes
Kleiderschrank, der . . . . . . clothes closet
klein, kleines . . . . small
Kleingeld, das . . . . . . small change, coins
Klingel, die . . . . doorbell
kocht/kochen . . . . cooks/to cook
Koffer, der . . . . suitcase
kommt/kommen . . . . comes/to come
Konditorei, die . . . . café
können . . . . to be able to, can
Konversation, die . . . . conversation
Konzert, das . . . . concert
Konzertkarte, die . . . . concert ticket
Kopfkissen, das . . . . pillow
kostet/kosten . . . . costs
Kotelett, das . . . . cutlet, chop
krank . . . . sick, ill
Krawatte, die . . . . tie
Kreis, der . . . . circle, district
Küche, die . . . . kitchen
kühl . . . . cool
Kühlschrank, der . . . . refrigerator
Kuli, der . . . . pen
kurz . . . . short

L

Laden, der (die Läden) . . . . . . store, shop
Lampe, die (die Lampen) . . . . lamp
landen . . . . to land
Landkarte, die . . . . map
lang . . . . long
langsam . . . . slow
langsamer . . . . slower
laut . . . . loud
Lebensmittelgeschäft, das . . . . . grocery store
leise . . . . soft
lernen . . . . to learn
lesen . . . . to read
Leute, die . . . . people

Licht, das ... light
Liegewagen, der ... reclining car
Likör, der ... liqueur
Linie, die (die Linien) ... line
linken ... left
links ... left
Liste, die ... list
Liter, der ... liter
Löffel, der ... spoon
los ... wrong

M

macht / machen ... makes / to make do
Mai, der ... May
man ... one
Mann, der ... man
Männer, die ... men
Mantel, der ... coat
Mark, die ... mark
Markstück, das ... mark piece
Markt, der ... market
Marktplatz, der ... market place
Marmelade, die ... jam
März, der ... March
mehr ... more
meine ... mine
Menü, das ... menu
Messer, das ... knife
Meter, der ... meter
Metzgerei, die ... butcher shop
Milch, die ... milk
Milchgeschäft, das ... dairy
mindestens ... at least
Mineralwasser, das ... mineral water
Minute, die (die Minuten) ... minute
mir ... to me, me
mit ... with
Mittagessen, das ... lunch
Mitte, die ... middle
Mittwoch, der ... Wednesday
möchte / möchten ... would like
Moment, der ... moment
Monat, der (die Monate) ... month
Montag, der ... Monday
morgen ... tomorrow
Morgen, der ... morning
morgens ... mornings
Münzfernsprecher, der ... coin-operated telephone
Museum, das ... museum
Museumplatz, der ... museum square
muß / müssen ... must / to have to
müssen ... to have to, must
Mutter, die ... mother

N

nach ... to, after
Nachmittag, der ... afternoon
nachmittags ... afternoons
Nachspeise, die ... dessert
nächst, nächsten ... next
Nacht, die ... night
Nachthemd, das ... nightshirt
Nachtisch, der ... dessert
Name, der (die Namen) ... name
neben ... next to
neblig ... foggy
nehmen ... to take
nein ... no
neu, neue, neuen ... new
neun ... nine
neunzehn ... nineteen
neunzig ... ninety
nicht ... no, not
nicht Raucher ... non-smoker
nicht wahr? ... isn't it so?
nichts ... nothing
niedrig ... low
noch ... still
Nord, der ... north
Norden, der ... north
nördlich ... northern
Notausgang, der ... emergency exit
November, der ... November
null ... zero
Nummer, die (die Nummern) ... number
nun ... now
nur ... only

O

oben ... above, upstairs
Obst, das ... fruit
Obstgeschäft, das ... fruit store
oder ... or
Ofen, der ... oven
offen ... open
öffnen ... to open
oft ... often
Oktober, der ... October
Omelett, das (die Omeletten) .. omelette
Onkel, der ... uncle
Oper, die ... opera
Opernhaus, das ... opera house
Orangensaft, der ... orange juice
Ortsgespräch, das ... local phone call
Ost, der ... east
Osten, der ... east
östlich ... eastern

P

packen ... to pack
Paket, das ... package
paniert ... breaded
Papier, das ... paper
Papierkorb, der ... wastepaper basket
Parkplatz, der ... parking space
parkt / parken ... parks / to park
Parterre, das ... ground floor
Paß, der ... passport
paßt / passen ... fits / to fit
Pension, die .. bed-and-breakfast lodging
Pensionzimmer, das ... room at a bed-and-breakfast
Personen, die ... persons
Personenzüge, die ... local trains
Pfeffer, der ... pepper
Pfennig, der (die Pfennige) ... pfennig
Pfund, das ... pound
Philosophie, die ... philosophy
Photo, das ... photograph
Platz, der ... space, place
Polizei, die ... police
Polizeiamt, das ... police station
Portion, die ... portion
Post, die ... mail
Postamt, das ... post office
Postkarte, die ... postcard
Preis, der (die Preisen) ... price
pro Stunde ... per hour
Problem, das (die Probleme) ... problem
Pulli, der (die Pullis) ... sweater
purpur ... purple

Q

Quelle, die ... source
Quittung, die ... receipt

R

R-Gespräch, das ... collect call
Rathaus, das ... city hall
Ratskeller, der ... city-hall restaurant
rauchen ... to smoke
Rauchen verboten ... smoking prohibited
Rasiermesser, das ... razor
Rechnung, die ... bill
rechten ... right
rechts ... right
Regenmantel, der ... raincoat
Regenschirm, der ... umbrella
regnet / regnen ... rains / to rain
reich ... rich
reinigt / reinigen ... cleans / to clean
Reinigung, die ... cleaners
Reise, die ... trip, travel
Reiseauskunft, die ... travel information
Reisebüro, das ... travel office
Reisekoffer, der ... trunk
reisen ... to travel
Reisewörter, die ... travel words
Religion, die (die Religionen) ... religion
Restaurant, das ... restaurant
Rettungsdienst, der ... rescue service
richtig, richtigen ... correct
Rind, das ... beef
Ritter, der ... knight
Rock, der ... skirt
Rolltreppe, die ... escalator
rosa ... pink
Rose, die (die Rosen) ... rose
rot ... red
Rotwein, der ... red wine

S

S-Bahn, die ... streetcar
sagt / sagen ... says / to say
Sahne, die ... whipped cream, cream
Salat, der (die Salate) ... salad
Salz, das ... salt
Samstag, der ... Saturday
Sandalen, die ... sandals
sauber ... clean
sauer ... sour
Schaffner, der ... conductor
Schalter, der ... counter
Scheck, der ... check
Schein, der (die Scheine) ... bank note
Schiff, das ... ship
Schinken, der ... ham
Schlafanzug, der ... pajamas
schlafen ... to sleep
Schlafwagen, der ... sleeping car
Schlafzimmer, das ... bedroom
schlecht ... bad
schließen ... to close
Schloß, das ... castle
Schneider, der ... tailor
schneidet / schneiden ... cuts / to cut
schneit / schneien ... snows / to snow
schnell ... fast
Schnellimbiß, der ... quick refreshment bar
Schnellzug, der ... train
Schokolade, die ... chocolate
schön ... pretty
Schrank, der ... closet, cupboard
schreiben ... to write
Schreibtisch, der ... desk
Schreibwarenhandlung, die ... stationery store
Schuh, der (die Schuhe) ... shoe
schwarz ... black
Schwein, das ... pig, pork
Schweinekotelett, das ... pork chop
Schwester, die ... sister
Schwimmbad, das ... swimming pool
schwimmen ... to swim
sechs ... six
sechzehn ... sixteen
sechzig ... sixty
See, die ... sea
Seeblick, der ... sea view
Seereise, die ... ocean voyage
sehen ... to see
sehr ... very
Seife, die ... soap
Seite, die (die Seiten) ... page
Sekunde, die ... second
senden ... to send

September, der .... September
Serviette, die .... napkin
sie .... she, they
Sie .... you
sieben .... seven
siebzehn .... seventeen
siebzig .... seventy
sieht .... sees
sind / sein .... are / to be
singen .... to sing
sitzen .... to sit
so .... as
Socken, die .... socks
Sofa, das .... sofa
Sohn, der .... son
Sommer, der .... summer
Sonnenbrille, die .... sunglasses
Sonntag, der .... Sunday
Spanien, das .... Spain
Spanisch, das .... Spanish
spät .... late
später .... later
Speisekarte, die .... menu
Speisewagen, der .... dining car
Spezialität, die .... specialty
Spiegel, der .... mirror
Sport, der .... sport
sprechen .... to speak
Stadt, die (die Städte) .... city
Stadtmitte, die .... city center
Stadtplan, der .... city map
Stammbaum, der .... family tree
steht / stehen .... stands / to stand
steigen .... to climb
Stiefel, die .... boots
Stock, das .... floor
Straße, die .... street
Straßenbahn, die .... streetcar
Straßenbahnhaltestelle, die ... streetcar stop
Straßenschilder, die .... street signs
Strumpfe, die .... socks
Strumpfhose, die .... panty hose
Stück, das .... piece
Stuhl, der (die Stühle) .... chair
Stunde, die (die Stunden) .... hour
Süd .... south
Süden, der .... south
südlich .... southern
Suppe, die (die Suppen) .... soup
süß .... sweet
Süßwarenladen, der .... candy shop

T

Tabak, der .... tobacco
Tabakladen, der .... tobacco store
Tag, der (die Tage) .... day
Tagesgericht, das .... daily special
Tankstelle, die .... gas station
Tante, die .... aunt
Taschentuch, das .... handkerchief
Tasse, die (die Tassen) .... cup
tausend .... thousand
Tausendmarkschein, der . thousand-mark bill
Taxi, das .... taxi
TEE ..... Trans-European Express train
Tee, der .... tea
Telefon, das .... telephone
Telefonanruf, der .... telephone call
Telefonbuch, das .... telephone book
Telefongespräch, das ..... telephone call
telefonieren .... to telephone
Telefonnummer, die .. telephone number
Telefonzelle, die .... telephone booth
Telegramm, das .... telegram
Teller, der .... plate
Temperatur, die .... temperature
Teppich, der .... carpet
teuer .... expensive
Theater, das .... theater
Theaterkarte, ... theater ticket
Tisch, der (die Tische) .... table
Toast, der .... toast
Tochter, die .... daughter
Toilette, die .... lavatory
Tomatensaft, der .... tomato juice
Tourist, der .... tourist
Treppe, die .... steps
trinken .... to drink
Tür, die .... door
typisch, typische .... typical

U

U-Bahn, die (die U-Bahnen) .... subway
U-Bahnfahrplan, der ... subway schedule
U-Bahnhaltestelle, die .... subway shop
über .... over, above
Überfall, der .... attack, accident
Uhr, die (die Uhren) .... clock, watch
Uhrmacher, der .... watchmaker
um .... around, at
umsteigen .... to transfer
und .... and
ungefähr .... approximately
uninteressant .... uninteresting
Universität, die .... university
unten .... below, downstairs
unter .... under
Unterhemd, das .... undershirt
Unterhose, die .... underpants
Unterrock, der .... slip

V

Vater, der .... father
Verb, das (die Verben) .... verb
verbinden .... to connect
verboten .... prohibited
Vereinigten Staaten, die .... the United States
vergessen .... to forget
verkaufen .... to sell
Verkehrsunfall, der ..... traffic accident
verlieren .... to lose
versch. .... abbre. for various
verstehen .... to understand
Verwandten, die .... relatives
viel .... much
viel Spaß .... much fun
viele .... many
vier .... four
Viertel, das .... quarter
vierzehn .... fourteen
vierzig .... forty
violett .... violet
voll .... full, drunk
vom (= von dem) .... from the
vom Hammel .... mutton
vom Kalb .... veal
vom Rind .... beef
vom Schwein .... pork
von .... from
vor .... in front of
Vorhang, der .... curtain
Vorname, der .... first name
vorsichtig .... careful
Vorspeisen, die .... hors d'oeuvres
Vorwahlnummer, die ... telephone prefix

W

Wagen, der .... car
wählen .... to dial
Wahlton, der .... dial tone
Wand, die .... wall
wann .... when
war .... was
Waren, die .... wares
Warenhaus, das ...... department store
warm .... warm
Wartesaal, der .... waiting room
warum .... why
was .... what
Waschbecken, das .... sink
waschen .... to wash
Wäscherei, die .... laundry
Waschlappen, der .... washcloth
wäscht / waschen ...... washes / to wash
Wasser, das .... water
Wechselstube, die.money-exchange office
wechselt / wechseln ...... exchanges / to exchange
Wecker, der .... alarm clock
Wein, der .... wine
Weinstube, die .... wine cellar
weiß / wissen .... knows / to know
weiß .... white
Weißwein, der .... white wine
weiter .... further
welche, welches, welchem .... which
wenig .... few
wer .... who
West, der .... west
Westen, der .... west
westlich .... western
Wetter, das .... weather
wichtig, wichtige .... important
wie .... how
Wie geht's? .... How are you?
wie lange .... how long
wieder .... again
wiederholen .... to repeat
wieviel .... how much
Wild, das .... venison
windig .... windy
Winter, der .... winter
wir .... we
wissen .... to know (a fact)
wo .... where
Woche, die (die Wochen) .... week
wohnen .... to live, reside
Wohnzimmer, das .... living room
Wort, das (die Wörter) .... word
Wörterbuch, das .... dictionary
Wurst, die .... sausage

Z

zahlen .... to pay
Zahnbürste, die .... toothbrush
Zahnpaste, die .... toothpaste
zehn .... ten
Zehnmarkschein, der ..... ten-mark bill
Zehnpfennigstück, das . ten-pfennig coin
Zentimeter, der .... centimeter
zeigen .... to show
Zeit, die .... time
Zeitschrift, die .... magazine
Zeitung, die .... newspaper
Zentrum, das .... center (of a city)
Zigarette, die .... cigarette
Zimmer, das .... room
Zoll, der .... customs
Zoo, der .... zoo
zu .... to, closed
Zug, der (die Züge) .... train
Zugfahrplan, der .... train schedule
Zugkarte, die .... train ticket
Zugreise, die .... train trip
zum (= zu dem) .... to the
zur (= zu der) .... to the
zur Sonne .... at the sun
zwanzig .... twenty
Zwanzigmarkschein, der .. twenty-mark bill
zwei .... two
Zweimarkstück, das ..... two-mark coin
Zweipfennigstück, das . two-pfennig coin
zweite Klasse .... second class
zwölf .... twelve

DRINKING GUIDE

This drinking guide is intended to explain the sometimes overwhelming variety of beverages available to you while in Germany. It is by no means complete. Some of the experimenting has been left up to you, but this should get you started. The asterisks (*) indicate brand names.

HEIßE GETRÄNKE (hot drinks)

Tasse Kaffee	cup of coffee
Portion/Kännchen Kaffee	pot of coffee
Glas Tee	cup of tea
(schwarz, Kamille)	(black, camomile)
Portion/Kännchen Tee	pot of tea
mit Zitrone	with lemon
mit Sahne	with cream
Glühwein	hot red wine with spices
Grog vom Rum	grog from rum

ALKOHOLFREIE GETRÄNKE (non-alcoholic drinks)

Fanta	Fanta
Cola	cola
Ginger Ale	ginger ale
Soda	club soda
Tonic Water	tonic water
Bitter Lemon	bitter lemon
Spezi	1/2 cola, 1/2 Fanta
Apfelsaft	apple juice
Orangensaft	orange juice
Tomatensaft	tomato juice
Traubensaft weiß	white grape juice
Johannisbeersaft schwarz	black currant juice
Milch	milk
Buttermilch	buttermilk
Orangenlimonade	orange drink
Zitronenlimonade	lemon-flavored drink
Mineralwasser	mineral water

SPIRITUOSEN (spirits)

Gin	gin
Rum	rum
Russischer Wodka	Russian vodka
Echter serbischer Slivovic	Serbian slivovic
Zwetschgenwasser	prune schnapps
Kirschwasser	cherry schnapps
Himbeergeist	raspberry schnapps
Williams-Birne	pear schnapps

***Obstler**
***Enzian**
***Doppelkorn**
***Doornkaat**

WHISKIES (whiskies)

This list has familiar names like Red Label, Black Label, Seagrams, etc. The Germans do have a clear whisky called **Korn** which is frequently ordered along with a **Bier.**

LIKÖRE (liqueurs)

Eierlikör	egg liqueur
Aprikot Brandy	apricot brandy
Kirschlikör	cherry liqueur

(and various other fruit liqueurs)

***Schwarzer Kater**
***Ettaler Klosterlikör**
***Drambuie**
***Cointreau**
***Grand Marnier**

HALBBITTER UND BITTER (bitters)

***Underberg**
***Jägermeister**
***Mampe Diktiner**

BIERE (beers)

There is a variety of brands. **Bier** is purchased in **Flaschen** (bottles) or **vom Faß** (draft).

Export vom Faß	draft export
Pils	pilsner
Diät-Pils	diet pilsner
Altbier	dark beer
Weizenbier	special wheat beer
Berliner Weiße (mit oder ohne Schuß- Waldmeister oder Himbeersirup)	Berlin specialty — beer (with or without a shot of **Waldmeister** or raspberry syrup)

WEINE (wines)

There are three main types and quality levels. **Wein** is purchased by the **Flasche** (bottle) or **offen** (open, like a house wine).

Rotwein	red wine
Weißwein	white wine
Rosé	rosé
Tafelwein	table wine
Qualitätswein	quality wine
Kabinettwein	choice wine
Eiswein	rare, special ice wine
Schorle	wine mixed with mineral water

The major wine-producing areas in **Deutschland** are

Baden	**Rheinhessen**
Mosel	**Neckar**
Rhein	**Franken**

APÊRITIFS UND SÜDWEINE (aperitifs)

Sherry	sherry
Portwein	port

***Pernod**
***Campari**
***Martini weiß**
***Martini rot**
(Not gin with an olive, but sweet vermouth! If you order a "martini," this is what you will get.)

COGNAC UND WEINBRAND (cognac)

***Remy Martin**
***Asbach Uralt**

SEKT UND CHAMPAGNER (champagne)

***Henkel**
***Kupferberg**

GUT IM SOMMER

Erdbeerbowle	champagne, white wine, strawberries
Pfirsischbowle	champagne, white wine, peaches

GUT IM WINTER

Feuerzangenbowle	red wine, orange slices, spices, sugar block coated with rum, flambé

Brot und Teigwaren (bread and pasta)

Brötchen	roll
Roggenbrot	rye bread
Schwarzbrot	Westphalian brown bread
Weißbrot	white bread
Nudeln	noodles
Spätzle	dumpling

Salate (salads)

Kopfsalat	lettuce
Bohnensalat	bean salad
Gemüsesalat	vegetable salad
Feldsalat	lamb's salad
Tomatensalat	tomato salad
Kartoffelsalat	potato salad
Endiviensalat	endive salad
Gurkensalat	cucumber salad
Selleriesalat	celery salad
Chikoreesalat	chicory salad
gemischter Salat	mixed salad
Geflügelsalat	chicken salad

Gemüse (vegetables)

Bohnen	beans
Erbsen	peas
Linsen	lentils
Spargel	asparagus
Karotten	carrots
Spinat	spinach
Lauch	leek
Tomaten	tomatoes
Pilze, Champignons	mushrooms
Weißkohl, Weißkraut	white cabbage
Rotkohl, Rotkraut	red cabbage
Blumenkohl	cauliflower
Rosenkohl	brussels sprouts
rote Beete, rote Rübe	beets
Mais	corn
Gurken	cucumbers
Kohlrabi	turnip-cabbage, kohlrabi
Zwiebeln	onions
Radieschen	radish (small, red kind)
Rettich	radish (big, white root)
Meerrettich	horseradish

Kartoffeln (potatoes)

gekochte Kartoffeln, Salzkartoffeln	boiled potatoes
Bratkartoffeln, Röstkartoffeln	fried potatoes
Kartoffelgemüse	potatoes in cream sauce
Kartoffelpüree, Kartoffelbrei	mashed potatoes
Pommes Frites	French fried potatoes
Kartoffelknödel	potato dumpling
Petersilienkartoffeln	parsley potatoes

Obst (fruit)

Apfel	apple
Birne	pear
Aprikose	apricot
Pfirsich	peach
Banane	banana
Orange, Apfelsine	orange
Mandarine	tangerine
Kirsche	cherry
Pflaume, Zwetschge	plum
Mirabelle	sweet, yellow plum
Apfelmus	applesauce
Kürbis	pumpkin
Melone	melon
Pampelmuse, Grapefruit	grapefruit
Kompott	stewed fruit
Traube	grape

Beeren (berries)

Erdbeere	strawberry
Himbeere	raspberry
Brombeere	blackberry
Stachelbeere	gooseberry
Johannisbeere (rot oder schwarz)	red or black currant
Preiselbeere	cranberry, red bilberry
Heidelbeere	blueberry

Guten Appetit!

die Speisekarte

menu

Art der Zubereitung (ways of preparation)

im Backteig	in batter
gekocht	cooked, boiled
gebraten	roasted, fried
gebacken	baked
gedämpft	steamed
geschmort	braised
gegrillt	grilled
paniert	breaded
roh - englisch	rare
kurz angebraten	medium-rare
durchgebraten	well-done

Allgemeines (general)

Marmelade	jam
Gelee	jelly
Honig	honey
Salz	salt
Pfeffer	pepper
Öl	oil
Essig	vinegar
Senf	mustard
Sosse	gravy
Aufschnitt	cold cuts
Käse	cheese
Nachtisch	dessert
Kuchen	cake
Gebäck	pastry
Eis	ice cream
Schlagsahne	whipped cream

Vorspeisen (hors d'oeuvres)

Austern	oysters
Gänseleber-Pastete	goose-liver pate
Heringsalat	herring salad
Italienischer Salat	Italian salad
Kaviar	caviar
Raucheraal	smoked eel
Russische Eier	Russian eggs
Weinbergschnecken	snails
Hummer-Cocktail	lobster cocktail
Froschschenkel	frog's legs

Suppen (soups)

Kraftbrühe mit Ei	clear soup with raw egg
Tagessuppe	soup of the day
klare Fleischbrühe	beef broth
Hühnerbrühe	chicken broth
Bohnensuppe	bean soup
Erbsensuppe	pea soup
Linsensuppe	lentil soup
Kartoffelsuppe	potato soup
Champignoncremesuppe	cream-of-mushroom soup
Ochsenschwanzsuppe	oxtail soup
Gulaschsuppe	Hungarian goulash soup
Schildkrötensuppe	turtle soup
Königinsuppe	cream-of-chicken soup

Eierspeisen (eggs)

ein weich gekochtes Ei	one soft-boiled egg
ein hart gekochtes Ei	one hard-boiled egg
Spiegelei	fried egg
Rührei	scrambled eggs
verlorenes Ei	poached egg
Omelett mit . . .	omelette with . . .
Bauernomelett	farmer's omelette
Strammer Max	open ham sandwich, fried egg on top

Fleisch (meat)

vom Kalb, Kalbfleisch (veal)

Kalbsbraten	roast veal
Kalbssteak	veal steak
Kalbsschnitzel	veal cutlet
Wiener Schnitzel	breaded veal cutlet

Fleisch (meat) continued

Paprika Schnitzel	red-pepper veal cutlet
Kalbskotelett	veal chop
Kalbsfrikassee	fricassee of veal
Kalbshaxe	shank of veal
Kalbskeule	leg of veal
gefüllte Kalbsbrust	stuffed breast of veal
Kalbsnierenbraten	loin of veal with kidneys
Kalbszunge	veal tongue
Kalbsleber	calf's liver
Kalbslendenbraten	filet of veal
Kalbsrollbraten	rolled veal roast

vom Rind (beef)

Rindfleisch-Ochsenfleisch	broiled beef
Rindersaftbraten	braised beef
Ochsenbrust	boiled brisket of beef
Lendensteak	loin steak
Deutsches Beefsteak	Salisbury steak
Gulasch	Hungarian goulash
Schmorbraten	pot roast
Ochsenzunge	beef tongue
Filetgulasch Stroganoff	beef Stroganoff
Rinderroulade	stuffed, rolled beef slices
Wiener Rostbraten	cube steak with fried onions

vom Schwein, Schweinefleisch (pork)

Schweinebraten	roast pork
Schweineschnitzel	pork steak
Schweinekotelett	pork chop
Schweinelendchen	pork filet
Schweinshaxe	pig's knuckles (fried)
Kassler Rippenspeer	saddle of pork
Schweineragout	ragout/stew
Hausmacher Bratwurst	homemade fried sausage
Eisbein	pig's knuckles (cooked)
Leberkäse	liver loaf
Schlachtplatte	hot pork sausages with sauerkraut

von Hammel, Hammelfleisch (mutton)

Hammelbraten	roast mutton
Hammelkotelett	mutton chop
Hammelkeule	leg of mutton
Lamm	lamb
Lammbraten	roast lamb

Geflügel (poultry)

Brathuhn	roast chicken
Hühnerfrikassee	chicken fricassee
Ente	duck
Gans	goose
Rebhuhn	partridge
Fasan	pheasant
Taube	pigeon
Truthahn/Puter	turkey

Wild (venison)

Hirschbraten	roast stag
Hirschsteak	steak of stag
Rehkeule	leg of roe deer
Rehbraten	roast venison
Rehlendenbraten	filet roast of venison
Hirschkeule	leg of deer
Wildschweinbraten	roast wild boar
Wildschweinsteak	wild-boar steak
Hasenkeule	leg of hare
Hasenrücken	saddle of hare
Hasenpfeffer	jugged hare

Fisch (fish)

Schellfisch	haddock
Scholle (Flunder)	flounder
Heilbutt	halibut
Forelle	trout (boiled/fried)
Goldbarschfilet	bass filet
Kabeljau	cod
Seezunge	sole
Makrele	mackerel
Hecht	pike
Muscheln	mussels
Krebse	crab
Krebsschwänze	freshwater shrimps
Karpfen	carp
Krabben	small shrimps
Ölsardinen	sardines (in oil)
Salm	salmon
Lachs/Raucherlachs	salmon/smoked salmon
Sardellen	anchovies
Aal	eel

(koh-men)
kommen

(high-sen)
heißen

(gay-en)
gehen

(kow-fen)
kaufen

(hah-ben)
haben

(shprek-en)
sprechen

(lair-nen)
lernen

(voh-nen)
wohnen

(murk-ten)
möchten

(be-stel-en)
bestellen

(brow-ken)
brauchen

(bly-ben)
bleiben

to be called	to come
to buy	to go
to speak	to have
to live/reside	to learn
to order	would like
to stay/remain	to need

(zah-gen) **sagen**	*(fair-kow-fen)* **verkaufen**
(es-sen) **essen**	*(zeh-en)* **sehen**
(trink-en) **trinken**	*(zen-den)* **senden**
(shtay-en) **stehen**	*(shlah-fen)* **schlafen**
(fair-shtay-en) **verstehen**	*(fin-den)* **finden**
(vee-dair-hoh-len) **wiederholen**	*(mah-ken)* **machen**

to sell

to see

to send

to sleep

to find

to do/make

to say

to eat

to drink

to stand

to understand

to repeat

(shry-ben)
schreiben

(lay-zen)
lesen

(tsigh-gen)
zeigen

(fahr-en)
fahren

(be-tsah-len) *(tsah-len)*
bezahlen/zahlen

(ar-by-ten)
arbeiten

(kur-nen)
können

(flee-gen)
fliegen

(mew-sen)
müssen

(zit-zen)
sitzen

(viss-en)
wissen

(pahk-en)
packen

to read	to write
to drive/travel	to show
to work	to pay
to fly	to be able to/can
to sit	to have to/must
to pack	to know

(bay-ginn-en) **beginnen**	*(bring-en)* **bringen**
(urf-nen) **öffnen**	*(shtai-gen)* **steigen**
(kohk-hen) **kochen**	*(ows-shtai-gen)* **aussteigen**
(lahn-den) **landen**	*(ine-shtai-gen)* **einsteigen**
(booh-ken) **buchen**	*(oom-shtai-gen)* **umsteigen**
(koh-sten) **kosten**	*(on-koh-men)* **ankommen**

to bring	to begin
to climb	to open
to get out	to cook
to get in	to land
to transfer	to book/reserve
to arrive	to cost

(ahp-fahr-en) **abfahren**	*(shlee-sen)* **schließen**
(ry-zen) **reisen**	*(vah-shen)* **waschen**
(rau-ken) **rauchen**	*(vex-zeln)* **wechseln**
(frah-gen) **fragen**	*(fair-lear-en)* **verlieren**
(es) (shnait) **es schneit**	*(eehk) (bin)* **ich bin**
(es) (rayg-net) **es regnet**	*(vir) (zint)* **wir sind**

to close

to depart

to wash

to travel

to exchange

to smoke

to lose

to ask

I am

it is snowing

we are

it is raining

(air) **er** (zee) **sie** } (ist) **ist** (es) **es**	(hohk) **hoch** - (nee-drig) **niedrig**
(zee) **Sie** (zint) **sind**	(ahrm) **arm** - (rike) **reich**
(zee) **sie** (zint) **sind**	(koorts) **kurz** - (long) **lang**
(owf) **Auf** (vee-dair-zeh-en) **Wiedersehen!**	(krahnk) **krank** - (ge-zoont) **gesund**
(es) **es** (gipt) **gibt**	(bil-ig) **billig** - (toy-air) **teuer**
(vee) **Wie** (gate) **geht** (es) **es** (ee-nen) **Ihnen?**	(ahlt) **alt** - (yoong) **jung**

high - low	he she } is it
poor - rich	you are
short - long	they are
sick - healthy	good-bye
cheap - expensive	there is/there are
old - young	How are you?

(goot) **gut** - *(shleckt)* **schlecht**	*(shnel)* **schnell** - *(long-zahm)* **langsam**
(ly-zah) **leise** - *(laut)* **laut**	*(dick)* **dick** - *(dewn)* **dünn**
(gross) **groß** - *(kline)* **klein**	*(feel)* **viel** - *(vay-nig)* **wenig**
(hice) **heiß** - *(kahlt)* **kalt**	*(owf)* **auf** - *(tsoo)* **zu**
(links) **links** - *(rex)* **rechts**	*(zeus)* **süß** - *(zow-air)* **sauer**
(oh-ben) **oben** - *(oon-ten)* **unten**	*(ent-shool-dee-goong)* **Entschuldigung!**

Sunset
Proof-of-Purchase
ISBN 0-944502-19-9

fast - slow

good - bad

thick - thin

soft - loud

much - little

large - small

open - closed

hot - cold

sweet - sour

left - right

excuse me

above - below